What people are saying about

The Embrace of Capital

So refreshing, and joyously subversive, to read a communist's analysis of why communism is so terribly unappetizing.
Yanis Varoufakis

Milligan offers a powerful left critique of the left; pointing to where it has gone wrong and some of the things that need to change...While not agreeing with every aspect of his analysis, he's right to identify two of the left's biggest failings: its inability to inspire the working class to support social transformation, and its lack of a detailed road map to secure its socialist vision.
Peter Tatchell

Genuinely thought provoking and provocative. A much-needed takedown of what Orwell once called the "smelly little orthodoxies" of the left, and why they are so distant and alienated from the working class they claim to fight for.
Ralph Leonard

Also by the author

The Politics of Homosexuality, 1973
ISBN 0902818325

Sex-Life: A Critical Commentary on the History of Sexuality, 1993
ISBN 0 7453 0611 X hb; ISBN 0 7453 0612 8 pb

The Truth About the Aids Panic, 1987
(Co-authored with Michael Fitzpatrick)
ISBN 094839207X pb

The Embrace of Capital

Capitalism from the Inside

The Embrace of Capital

Capitalism from the Inside

Don Milligan

zer0 books

Winchester, UK
Washington, USA

JOHN HUNT PUBLISHING

First published by Zero Books, 2022
Zero Books is an imprint of John Hunt Publishing Ltd., No. 3 East St., Alresford,
Hampshire SO24 9EE, UK
office@jhpbooks.com
www.johnhuntpublishing.com
www.zero-books.net

For distributor details and how to order please visit the 'Ordering' section on our website.

ISBN: 978 1 78904 801 8
978 1 78904 802 5 (ebook)
Library of Congress Control Number: 2021936362

A CIP catalogue record for this book is available from the British Library.

Design: Stuart Davies

UK: Printed and bound by CPI Group (UK) Ltd, Croydon, CR0 4YY
Printed in North America by CPI GPS partners

Contents

For Sandra

Preface

This book is a development of two short pieces written in June 2020, "Communists facing up to reality," and "Capitalism: a fully functioning society," both published in 'Articles' at www.donmilligan.net. It is about our love-hate relationship with capitalism. The book attempts to identify the reasons why we on the left, near and far, have failed so conspicuously to persuade working people to put an end to commercial society. It could not have been written without the encouragement, criticism, and support of Sean Dower, Jonathan Milligan, Shabaaz Mohammed, Ann Morphew, Mick Owens, Cat Rylance, Joanna Thornberry, and Rachel Twaites. I must give special thanks to Chris Strafford and Billy Griffiths for their patient arguments and criticism, which revealed disagreements, that have made the book considerably more coherent than it might otherwise have been.

Don Milligan, January 2021

Introduction

Dismay and Disdain

I well remember the dismay of the comrade charged with getting me through volume one of Karl Marx's magnum opus, *Capital: A Critique of Political Economy*. The *Capital* Reading Group met in the party offices, in the stark chill of the Political Committee's room, where the leaders at other important moments orchestrated the life of the party. Over several weeks of evening meetings, we plowed on through the great tome. It's a difficult read, needing much explanation of novel concepts and neologisms at every page or two. It's a process rather like employing the major and minor arcana needed to understand the signifiers of a Tarot spread. Consequently, I kept raising ticklish questions which took us way beyond the text and revealed a bewildering difference in our approach to thinking about capitalism. This came to a head during a discussion of advertising, which I insisted was part of the "production process"; the production of "surplus value," that is, not of the "commodity" itself.

This led me off at a tangent to an expression of my delight at various adverts, particularly one set in Smarties Place, an imaginary night club for kids, a pale vanilla nod to *Bugsy Malone*, in which 10-year-olds were served cocktail glasses full of multicolored chocolate Smarties. The boys and girls were deliriously happy. The copywriters had come up with the line, "Things are happening at Smarties Place." Evidently, they were building on Rowntree Mackintosh's enigmatic slogan, "Only Smarties have the answer."

My delight in describing the ad invited an expression of confused disdain. I became aware, and not for the first time, of the almost unbridgeable gulf between my puritanical earnestness, and my desire for indulgence and the ridiculous. This had been the case since I was 15 or 16 in the Young Communist League. It took many years for me to realize that the earnestness and gravitas, to which we all aspired, created an almost impermeable barrier between us communists, and an ordinary encounter with the culture of capitalism. There was always the big gap between what we revolutionaries were supposed to feel about capitalism, and my enjoyment of luxurious spectacle, conspicuous consumption, and the superabundance of entertaining fripperies, which abound in the "free world."

A sharp example of this tension between my triviality, and the gravity of our fight against the bosses, had surfaced a year before our discussion of advertising. It was over the marriage of Prince Charles to the aristocrat, Lady Diana Spencer. Now, as a communist and confirmed republican, I was enchanted by the spectacle. I avidly took in every detail from the television broadcast along with the better part of a billion other people around the world, including the couple of million people who crowded into central London for the shindig.

My comrades were left cold by the spectacle of almost 8 meters of silk taffeta spreading down the steps of St Paul's Cathedral. Diana's ivory silk dress, richly embellished with embroidery, sequins, and ten thousand pearls, left them thinking only about the waste, the extravagance, and the cost. This dismal thought was cheerfully banished by hundreds of thousands of people cheering and waving flags from Clarence House on The Mall, along The Strand and Fleet Street, up Ludgate Hill, to the steps of St Paul's. A jubilant crush, seven or eight deep on both sides of the street, cheered and clapped the procession of high-stepping horses, gorgeous carriages, and grand personages the whole way. People also packed the windows of offices along the route from Admiralty Arch to the Cathedral.

The milling masses seemed to like the gilded flummery, the

rather mad tufted tricorn hats, glittering with gold wire and tassels, adorning the heads of the footmen and "bullet catchers" standing on the back of the principal carriages. Nobody, apart from my comrades, seemed that concerned about faux medieval social hierarchies, the gilded eighteenth-century outfits, the little posh boys dressed as Victorian midshipmen, or the maids of honor with flowers in their hair. The brazen inequality on display did not disturb. I imagine that the million or so packing the streets, enjoying their participation in "a moment of history," were the same people who deal with unfairness and inequality every day, live with contradictions, make nice distinctions, and appear to be unfazed by inconsistency and meandering thoughts about the magic of royalty, and the tourist dollars drawn in by monarchical pageantry.

> *This, in a nutshell, is what we call false consciousness*
> Rose in Upstairs at the Party, Linda Grant

Revolutionary socialists shouted "Stuff the Wedding" and were more or less ignored by the populace at large, including even those utterly uninterested in the right royal carry-on. There were millions of them scattered throughout Britain – they didn't cheer or clap or wave the Union Jack – but they could spare no time for republican protests or "stuffing the wedding" either. They simply ignored it, went to the pub, to the shops, or down the allotment, as if nothing was happening.

So the right royal circus was hugely enjoyed and hugely pleasurable. The communists and the left were decidedly out of step with almost all sections of the public. The subsequent divorce, extramarital affairs, Her Majesty's *Annus Horribilis* in 1992, the death of Diana 5 years later, the great recession of 2007-2009, Brexit, and the pandemic have not altered the fortunes of those who want to transform or overthrow the system in any decisive manner. Through all our ups and downs our culture of acceptance and participation is undimmed.

Of course, there are those who will point to the popularity of vast gatherings and pageants organized by state authorities in the old Soviet Union, or East Germany, but such gatherings were organized by party "cells," and committees of communist party members, embedded in every workplace and neighborhood. Nothing was left to chance in striving for maximum public involvement in waving banners and cheering the parades and mobile tableaux designed to celebrate the achievements of the dictatorship.

In complete contrast, the popularity of the fake medieval rigmarole associated with the monarchy in Britain is elaborately "spontaneous." To be sure, royal events are canvassed by press and television for weeks or even months ahead, and trade upon the fact that more than 70 percent of the population love the Queen. Despite widespread criticism of "minor royals" and "hangers on," monarchical institutions are wildly popular, and do not need the state to sanction or "require" attendance of the general public at royal weddings, funerals, and coronations.

This book is about how confusing and difficult it is to pin down exactly what capitalism is all about. It is also an attempt to fathom exactly how the revolutionary or communist left, call them what you will, has largely misread and underestimated the depth and tensile strength of capitalist culture. There is a deep historical irony at work here, because Karl Marx himself was no slouch when it came to understanding that the rise of the industrial bourgeoisie played havoc with venerable cultural assumptions, and practices. He has been followed over the years by many intellectuals on the left, most notably Walter Benjamin and Antonio Gramsci, who made major contributions on the emergent culture of capitalism.[1] To this must be added the rich vein of historical writing pioneered by left-wing historians, particularly in France and Britain, that has greatly enhanced our understanding of the day-to-day lives of peasants, serfs, slaves, and artisans in the past.[2]

Yet this work has failed to inform in any vivid or practical way the trajectory of most socialist thought about capitalism, because forms of economism, shorn of Marxism's wider resources, have always dominated the movement.[3] Although most people would freely acknowledge that capitalism is "a mode of life," as well as "a mode of production," the tendency on the left to see the latter, but not the former, explains and sustains our failure.

This is because it is *de rigueur* among socialists to be gripped by thoughts of waste and superficiality. They march in step with Andy Sachs's first encounter with the world of high fashion in the movie *The Devil Wears Prada*. Haute Couture, its subtlety and the mesh of fine distinctions which hold it together, is simply absurd. It is akin to advertising, in this socialist schema, to see these luxurious things as wasteful epiphenomena, skin deep; they stand in for all that would be radically unnecessary in a well-ordered society.

This emerges from a socialist or anti-capitalist orthodoxy saturated by the study of economic relations and thoughts about the nature of exploitation. These are concerns which give rise immediately to an overriding interest in equality and justice – indeed in this egalitarian mood the mainstream left moves some way beyond Marxism in believing that "equality" and "justice" amount to the same thing. Their mantra being that there can be no justice without equality. As a result, capitalism is seen as a mode of production that spontaneously gives rise to a mode of life rooted in inequality and injustice. Although most socialists understand that inequality is not new or recent, capitalism is arraigned for perpetuating and maybe even intensifying injustice.

As a consequence, socialists and communists aspire to the moral high ground, in which political charity is lavished on the poor and disadvantaged, although actual charitable works remain largely the preserve of community-minded folk with little or no connection with left-wing politics. This is because most left-wingers believe that what is done by charities should be done by the authorities. Oscar Wilde's Christian-socialist disdain for charity, along with his celebration of the ungrateful, undeserving, rebellious poor, is largely forgotten by red-hot socialists, who invariably argue that all welfare should be provided by an almighty state.[4]

This kind of focus springs from an overriding concern with matters economic and a historical focus upon the development of economic and class relations seen through the prism of wealth and poverty, excess and want. It has a one-dimensional note in which the buoyant and irreducible desire for the enjoyment of a multitude of consumer goods found among the population at large is thought of as reprehensible. The socialist desire for what Raymond Williams, in the fifties and sixties, called "common-sharing" is regarded as the proper or meaningful aspiration among those who understand what is really and truly wrong with capitalism.

Competition and the pursuit of profit, above all else, results in sharpened conflict both at home and abroad. On the level of international relations, capitalism is thought of as a system in which competition for resources and markets leads, perhaps inevitably, to war in which working people are dragooned against their real interests to fight and die for those who exploit them in the drive "for the self-expansion of capital." In complete contrast, "peace and socialism" are like Doris Day's "love and marriage," thought to go together, like a "horse and carriage." Whereas capitalism is intrinsically warlike, constantly straining at the limits of national boundaries in the struggle for greater and greater profits, socialism is committed to what used to be called "the brotherhood of man," and is now figured more inclusively as "human solidarity."

This superior grasp which socialists have on the nature of

the existing state of affairs gives rise, automatically, to the perpetuation of the notion of "false consciousness." People who disagree with us, or fail to view capitalism in the correct manner, are gripped with venal concerns for the retention of their monied privileges, or as is much more common, are simply jogging along under the malign influence of false consciousness. The ideological domination of society by the well-to-do is said to undermine the capacity of most working people for critical thought and action. If only these benighted souls could, like socialist intellectuals, understand the true nature of "bourgeois cultural hegemony," all would be well, and another world would be possible.

So "the capitalist system" has a solid and well-defined character on the socialist and communist left. The "system" is an idea that has real substance, like something made of granite, marble, and iron, a thing unmistakable, well defined, fashioned into definite shapes, recognizable to all who care to look and to know. There are, of course, manifold differences among socialists. Some think of the system as a thing in which the 1 percent of the super-rich is pitted against the 99 percent. Others take a broader view, conceiving of the system as one of international corporations battening on the planet, shaping and laying it waste, in the pursuit of the bottom line. All socialists are united in the sense that although capitalism has produced unimaginable wealth and prosperity, it is intrinsically unable to distribute these wonders equally to all and sundry. Consequently, it is a system given over to injustice, and as such, must be done away with.

This book is a discussion of the way in which socialists and communists have walled themselves up within their own take on things, which has made it difficult, if not impossible, for them to discuss how capitalism has spontaneously embrewed a rich culture of acceptance, participation, and inclusion, that has doomed its opponents in bourgeois democratic states to the margins for almost 2 centuries.

In France and Italy, extremely large communist parties supported the idea of free trade unions and democratic rights, while they steadfastly supported dictatorship in countries where their sister parties were actually in power.[5] Consequently, they aligned their brand of socialism with a conception of modernity which was frankly dictatorial.[6] In Britain this also included the Communist Party of Great Britain regularly sending the minutes of its central committee to Moscow. Following the Hungarian Revolution of 1956, the CPGB also accepted substantial payments in cash from the dictatorship funneled through the Soviet Embassy in London.[7] Indeed, as a youngster selling *Challenge*, the paper of the Young Communist League, and the Communist *Daily Worker* on London's Kilburn High Road in 1959 and 1960, workers passing by would routinely shout "Go Back to Russia" while taunting us about "Moscow Gold," which, of course, we would indignantly reject. The idea of our party secretly taking money sent from the Soviet Union was, as far as we were concerned, simply absurd.

So we have a tradition on the left that has failed to account for the manner in which the great majority of people in capitalist society live within its contradictions, and find the socialist description of their lives – the left's angry indignation and superior consciousness – distinctly unappealing – ranged as it is against the way they choose to live, and the settlements they've felt able to make.

Most people do not feel either confused or selfish about the way they live. They think that their consciousness is just fine. Well-being is insisted upon, alongside a homological reality in which depression and poor mental health abounds as those with fewer resources face utility bills they can't pay, and toys they can't afford to buy for their kids. These pressures sit beside and, in some senses confirm, the common view that capitalism is produced by natural impulses toward self-advancement, and to the reproduction of inequality, which most people regard as a natural, if unattractive, aspect of the way things are. They do not identify with the socialist left's ideas about class.

Although millions of people are well aware that things are stacked against them, and apart from preferring the Labour Party to the Tories, they cannot see any compelling reason to want communists to overthrow the system. They are deeply unconvinced by the socialist dream of a better tomorrow; they fear a world in which private capital has been banished and "human solidarity" or "the brotherhood of man" has been declared compulsory by a socialist state. They fear the unfreedom bound up with the socialist ideal of equality and justice for all, which has up until now always been the harbinger of tyranny and dictatorship.

This introduction leads on to a detailed discussion on the emergence and nature of capitalism in the next chapter. The reason for this change of gear is to start by disentangling what might be meant by "capitalism" and the "capitalist system," from the vague, but irate, indignation of those who see exploitation and oppression everywhere. In line with their predilections, prejudices, and shibboleths, many socialists attempt to attribute all that ails the world to the greed of capitalists and "the violence of the system."

One is reminded of Reg's rhetoric in *The Life of Brian* about the Romans: "They've bled us white, the bastards. They've taken everything we had, and not just from us, but from our fathers, and our father's father...And what have they ever given us in return?" The answer is, of course, "rather a lot." The same might be said of the capitalist class as we turn to a fuller account of the "system."

Chapter 1

The Hall of Mirrors

Hauling two bags of shopping up Market Street in Manchester, I sat down for a short rest and found myself facing a branch of Foot Locker. The screens in the shop window boldly told me that "Shoes Don't Change the World – You do!" The next piece of novel information from the multinational Venator Group[1] was: "Change the world from what it is, to what it should be." This was followed by the assertion that "Black Lives Matter," accompanied by a sexy white girl waving a rainbow flag.

All very confusing, until I reflected on my childhood in London in the late forties and early fifties. At primary school we'd all queue up every day, each clutching a tablespoon we'd brought from home. Then, one-by-one, we were allowed to scoop out a delicious spoonful of malt from a big stone jar, closely supervised by our teacher. The malt was supplemented by a third of a pint of milk, free, every day. This government largesse came via the London County Council, along with free concerts and film shows in our local park, and a full-time attendant, Mrs Bowes, at the swings and sand pits. She had a small room that she could boil a kettle in and make tea, and deal with the minor injuries we suffered from time to time. Predictably enough, we would taunt her as "Mrs Bones." The old lady would then oblige by chasing us, sweeping her long litter-spike on the ground which threw up showers of dancing sparks. Of course, she never caught us, and we were always immediately forgiven.

So life in capitalist society has always been appalling, confusing, contradictory, and full of fun.

Like most people, I didn't really become conscious of capitalism until I started full-time employment. For me this momentous event took place in 1960, when I was 15, and started work as a messenger at a commercial art studio in London's Soho. The studio's owner was a woman who employed a dozen men, who used air-brushes to improve or alter photographs, and a couple of lettering artists. She had iron-gray hair, was usually dressed entirely in black, and constantly smoked cigarettes in a long holder which she flourished to emphasize her precise instructions. She had a whiskey voice, and was rarely gainsaid, as she ran the business with great aplomb. This woman was my first capitalist. To me, she was astonishing, exotic; I'd never encountered such a person before.

I had no idea how anything worked. I just ran about taking large black artwork bags to and from advertising agencies in Mayfair. I was well-paid, weekly, in cash. After I'd handed over two pounds to my mum, I had five pounds a week for fares, lunches, clothes, coffee bars, the pictures, and beer, more than enough for a young lad. Despite being a member of the Young Communist League, and the treasurer of the local Youth Campaign for Nuclear Disarmament, I knew nothing about profits, exploitation, or commerce. I had no idea how the posh people who appeared to orchestrate the world around me, did what they did.

This didn't stop me having all kinds of opinions about the evils of capitalism, or going on demonstrations about faraway places I found difficult to find on a map. Accordingly, in 1961, I did mark the execution of Patrice Lumumba[2] by imperialist-backed forces, by marching to the Belgian Embassy, along with the other habitués of the Partisan Coffee House on Soho's Carlisle Street. This was my first brush with police horses and a spot of low-level rioting. Soon, I was a clerk at Sanderson's Wallpaper on Berners Street. Above the time-clock in the staff entrance there was an illuminated scroll bearing the names of employees who'd worked for the firm for 25 years, and no longer had to clock-in. I suspect the prospect of life-long servitude was meant to be tantalizing; I found it frankly terrifying, and didn't last long in the Pattern Book Department, sacked for truculence and bad time-keeping after a few months.

I imagine that capitalism continues to remain something of a mystery, to this day, for most people entering the labor market. It's not clear that the jumble of banks, supermarkets, hairdressers, nail bars, offices, factories, car showrooms, and repair shops, within which we work, can be called a system, but it does seem to be all about commerce, buying and selling more or less anything, as fast as possible. And it is not until we get our first job that we enter fully into this market place, working for money, in return for the time and energy we spend at work.

So we find ourselves inside what Adam Smith called "commercial society." This is a world in which most things are made, sown, or harvested in order to be sold on to other people, anywhere they're buying. Before the emergence of this kind of commerce, most things were made for local use and consumption, by farm laborers and artisans, growing and making stuff for themselves, their families, and their near neighbors to use. So the change that occurred in the Netherlands during the early years of the seventeenth century, and a bit later in England, was ground-breaking. For the first time, the life of two whole populous countries began to be determined and configured by trade – more and more things were produced, not for local use, but to sell. Buying and selling took hold, as Holland and England began to ship goods to and from the ends of the Earth.[3]

Trade has, of course, always been important since ancient times. For example, the Neolithic people at Grimes Graves in Norfolk, England, dug out vast quantities of flint to make into tools around 4000 years ago.[4] They produced so much that they must have traded these flints over long distances. In the early medieval, ninth and tenth centuries, seafarers from Denmark and Sweden traded in furs, amber, and slaves, from Dublin to Constantinople. Much later, during the Renaissance in mainland Europe, cities like Venice and Florence also engaged in extensive trade, and this dominated the lives and purposes of their laborers and craftsmen, despite their society being saturated with military and religious obligations that constantly undermined the money-making, marketing, and commerce of princely rulers and city assemblies of wealthy men.

Similar trajectories of development seem to have characterized commercial life in China and Japan for many centuries. Although both countries, like many other parts of the world, had for hundreds of years developed highly sophisticated commercial arrangements with regard to agricultural and artisanal activity, capitalism did not arise. Traditional military, imperial, aristocratic, and social arrangements, together with associated cultural and philosophical assumptions, appear to have acted as a barrier to the relentless pursuit of growth that in the fulness of time came to be known globally as "modernity."

However, caution is required concerning the kind of historical certainty that has arisen regarding the pre-eminence of European experience. Bin Wong's observation is well made:

> When we take European developments as the norm, all other experiences appear to be abnormal. We begin to search for what went wrong in other parts of the world.[5]

This is of course true, but the empirical evidence of the spread, from the sixteenth century onwards, of commercial society associated with Western European ideas of "limitless" growth and "unending" innovation is overwhelming.

Indeed, one year after Columbus had made landfall in 1492 in what are now known as the Bahamas, the Pope issued a papal bull speculatively conferring all the lands that might be discovered west of a north-south meridian, drawn around 420 kilometres[6] west of the Cape Verde Islands, to Spain, and all those to the east of the line to Portugal. A year later in 1494 Spain and Portugal agreed in the Treaty of Tordesillas to shift the line around a thousand kilometers to the west – this gave the territory of what was to become Brazil to Portugal.

Within a century Portugal was engaging in extensive trade, not primarily with the Americas, but with merchants in India, through outposts in what is now Indonesia, and on islands off the coast of China. By 1600 the Dutch were doing all they could to pillage Portuguese ships of their cargoes of silk and porcelain from Jingdezhen. By the early years of the seventeenth century trade between Europe and China (with or without the permission of the Imperial Court) began to flourish. Clearly, considerable sums of Chinese merchant capital were involved in conveying goods to the coast for sale to European merchantmen. Yet this trade, although extensive, did not create commercial relations that went much beyond local or regional centers in China, or delivering luxuries to the Forbidden City in Beijing.

So while what was going on in Holland and England in the seventeenth century was not, strictly speaking, unique or new, what was different, and really novel, was the extent of the trade, and the way in which it directly shaped agricultural production and manufacturing, across numerous Dutch and English farms and towns. This involved wide swathes of farmland in both countries being cleared, drained, and made ready to provide foodstuffs for growing urban populations, and producing raw materials needed by artisans and manufacturers. This was the beginning of capitalism in which merchants became important, and by the end of the seventeenth century and the beginning of the eighteenth, traders and money-men actually assumed the leadership of government and society, in the Netherlands and England.[7]

Of course, society didn't change overnight. Despite revolutions in government, agricultural techniques, banking, publishing, the press, and the invention, toward the end of the eighteenth century, of steam-driven machines in England, elements of the old ways of doing things survived long into the nineteenth century. The situation of agricultural laborers, children, and young people in workshops and mines often found them bound to their parents who, in effect, were their employers. The head of the household would be given a price for the job in hand, and he would enlist the help of his wife and children to complete the task whatever it was. This situation began to pass away as manufacturing began increasingly to take place in large workshops and factories. Workers would, often for the first time, be hired as individuals and work under the surveillance of factory owners and their overlookers. This increased supervision, and the imposition of industrial discipline, made work much more intense and onerous. However, and perhaps paradoxically, it widened the freedom of workers, because when they were not at work, they were free to live as they pleased and their resources permitted. Methodism, and other non-conformist religious initiatives, together with freer relations between young men and women began to undermine the passivity of the laboring classes so earnestly desired by traditional elites. Workers began to exert their independence not only in matters of religion, but also in their views of society. They began to organize trade unions in order to compel masters to improve pay and conditions, and political clubs to discuss how working men could achieve representation and the vote.

During the alarm raised by the French Revolution of 1789 and the subsequent Terror in France, the government in London sought to contain and smother emerging radical elements among artisans and the laboring classes with the suppression of *habeas corpus* for a year in 1794, and the seizure of the papers of the London Corresponding Society, together with the arrest and imprisonment of John Thelwall, and of the Corresponding Society's secretary, Thomas Hardy. Fears of revolutionary conspiracies also led William Pitt's government to attempt the dissolution of labor organizations with "An Act to prevent Unlawful Combinations of Workmen" in 1799.[8] This act, also known as the Combination Act, was designed to ban trade unions and protect masters from their workers' attempts to force them into collective bargaining over wages and conditions. It remained in force until 1824, only to be replaced by a similarly draconian law aimed at crushing strikes and greatly restricting trade union organization. In this way, the state sought to impose upon urban workers similar conditions of servitude they'd experienced under the heel of the farmer, the landlord, the magistrate, and the parson in their ancestral villages.[9] That the authorities were not universally successful was revealed by the emergence of mass movements among working people over the need to raise wages, restrict the use of machines, limit working hours, and in support of political rights, including the right of working men to vote.[10]

Even mill owners and other capitalists were denied effective political rights as the old landed oligarchy attempted to hang onto the reins of power. For example, some large industrial towns in England found that they continued to be ruled over by "lords of the manor" until 1835,[11] and imprisonment for debt in Britain lasted until 1869.[12] However, all sorts of things associated with the ancient past, like monarchy, aristocratic titles – dukes, marquesses, and earls – were given new meaning, as the great and the good earned more money from investing in slaves in the Caribbean, or in industry at home – buying and selling – than they ever did by living off rents from the farmers and laborers on their estates.[13]

So the commercial society described, analyzed, and criticized by Adam Smith, David Ricardo, Karl Marx, and others continued to be as confusing to most people as it does today. Adam Smith talked about the division of labor, David Ricardo worried about the source of value, Karl Marx wrote polemical chapter and verse about the bourgeoisie, bourgeois society, and the commodity, while James Mill talked about international trade and "comparative advantage."[14] A myriad of theories have arisen in efforts to catalog and understand the society we live in today, and which those of a theoretical bent, now call "the capitalist system."

One problem is that it is not at all clear how systematic the capitalist system is. If the word "system" means a set of things working together as parts of a complex whole, or of an interconnecting network, then the capitalist system is composed of a great many things that cannot be considered capitalist. Large parts of the economy are run by the state and local authorities, other bits are not-for-profit enterprises, like the building societies that decided not to become banks;[15] charities and a host of other activities do not appear to have anything at all to do with commerce, capitalism, or making money, rather than "raising it." This is even true of elite institutions like public schools, and of most private healthcare insurance in the UK.[16]

In 2019 there were just under 168,000 charities in the UK with a combined income of around £10 billion. Of these organizations, 2356 each had an income of more than £5 million a year.[17] For example, in 1824 the national institution for the preservation of life from shipwreck was founded, and became the Royal National Lifeboat Institution in 1860. Its 238 lifeboat stations, 444 lifeboats, 4600 crew members, and 3000 shore and station support staff are maintained entirely by donations, investments, charitable trading, and other fund-raising activities, which pull in around £190 million a year.[18]

Then there is the "private life" of families and all the work of child rearing, and the voluntary care for the infirm and elderly. Most of which is done by women, without payment or the involvement of employers. Indeed, it is possible to argue that by far the greatest amount of work carried out in capitalist society is not carried out for commercial reasons at all, but for love, a sense of social obligation, or a powerful commitment to the communities in which people live.

Clearly capitalism would not be possible at all without this enormous amount of non-capitalist activity. By and large our social and cultural infrastructure is not provided within the realm of commerce. Some theorists overcome this problem by simply including all unpaid labor in the processes of capital accumulation and exploitation, by the "capitalist class in general," of the "working class in general." But, to most of us, family life and charitable endeavor does not appear to have anything much to do with capitalism. Yet despite all this, commerce does continue to dominate our lives in the manner first noticed by writers in the seventeenth and eighteenth centuries.

"Systemic" it may not be, but "determining" it most certainly is. Commerce, and the drive to make the profits necessary to keep a business running, creates the matrix within which everything else happens. The kinds of employment available, and the styles of life associated with our jobs, the character of our neighborhoods, cities, towns and villages, are largely shaped, developed, and redeveloped by commerce and commercial interests. The books we read, the movies we watch, the computer games we play, the music we listen to, and most of the theatrical performances we will ever see have been produced in commercial settings, if not for commercial reasons.

Here's another confusion. Authors may want to get paid for their books, scores, screenplays, and theater pieces, but they do not do what they do for commercial reasons. Anymore than the *Rolling Stones* continue their life-long touring across the globe because they either need or want the money they get paid. They're aging rock musicians that simply refuse to surrender to the ravages of time. People's personal motivations can rarely be contained or understood from a purely mercenary point of view. Even Bob Dylan's decision to start painting and selling prints cannot really be driven by any commercial impulse.

To be sure the famous and celebrated are surrounded by agents and a money-making apparatus that determine a great deal of what happens, but it cannot be said that the commercial flurry in which they live determines the motivation of the artists in question.

This applies to most businessmen and proprietors too. Whether a person starts a bakery or a plumbing business, a shipping and logistics company, or a financial consultancy is always driven by their biographies, their particular skills, experiences, personal relationships, interests, and aspirations. It is these that direct them into their chosen fields, every bit as much as the desire to make money or to succeed commercially. This is because the ownership of capital is always entangled in the life chances and choices of the capitalist. Capital does not come into the world as an orphan, it is not without family connections, and family commitments.

If capital is a "relation" as the straitlaced Marxists say – not an inherent quality of money, machines, or equipment – but a quality acquired by things, when they are used in "the self-expansion of capital," or to put it more simply, to make profits, then capital is not vested in physical objects, but in the relation between things and people. This, I think, is broadly true, and can give us little or no insight into the life or behavior of the capitalist.

Most capitalists are engaged in relatively small businesses, with a dozen or so employees, usually less, sometimes more, but rarely have more than a hundred people on the payroll. They are engaged in hiring and firing their staff, in running the business, and take an active day-to-day part in whatever it is their firm has been set up to make or provide. This gives them an intimate knowledge and understanding of their business, and with the staff they pay to work in it. Big capitalists, those with many hundreds of employees, are compelled to run their firms with the help of elaborate networks of managers or franchise owners which move them some way beyond the front-line of manufacturing or service provision.

However, they are not as remote as what might be called the *rentier* or "passive" capitalists who simply invest their money in stocks and bonds and live off the income. In a sense these people are renting out their fortune, bank balances, capital, call it what you will, to the "active" capitalists, in return for dividends. They are the "passive" capitalists who take no part in the daily grind of running stores, factories, repair shops, cafes, offices, or banks. Like good landlords, they simply maintain the property and collect the rents. They are served by a professional caste of money-men, brokers, asset managers, and financial advisors, who are often investors themselves, and in this sense must be counted among the capitalists.

Consequently, capitalists come in many variegated forms, from the majority of hard-working day-to-day proprietors of small and medium enterprises, that employ around half the employed population, all the way up to the moguls who own and run multinational corporations, and the mass of *rentiers*, or "passive" capitalists, idly taking their cut.

This means that capitalists rarely conform to the caricature beloved by many people on the left. Capitalists are often hard-working folk who've risked their own homes and mortgages in order to bankroll their businesses. They know their workers well, and are mortified if they are forced to lay-off staff in lean times. They strive to increase their turnover to the degree that will permit their bankers to provide them with overdraft facilities, enabling them to pay wages and overheads, even when there are delays in incoming payments for services and goods already provided to their customers. Maintaining cashflow is their perennial concern, a veritable nightmare at the end of every month.

This is a far cry from the world of Elon Musk or Bill and Belinda Gates, who live in the capitalist stratosphere, far above the world of most business owners, who remain firmly stuck to the surface of the system. This adds a further layer of confusion to how most of us encounter commercial society. It certainly doesn't seem like a system, and it doesn't seem that all the men and women who own and run businesses are bastards that we should hate on sight. On the contrary, most of them seem like ordinary people, sometimes good, sometimes bad, sometimes truly appalling, but as much concerned with making a living as the rest of us.

Most capitalists seem to be as much the victims of remote, unseen, and powerful forces as the people they employ. They have to deal with globalization – vast flows of investment that sweep around the world, intensifying competition and reducing prices in ways that create unending headaches for those running businesses in relatively high-wage economies. This is because, despite the fact that most businesses are "medium" or "small," the commercial space in which they operate is shaped, determined, or controlled by vast business corporations that employ the other half of those employed in most economies around the world.

This reality puts the terms of trade well beyond the control of most of the capitalist class. They have little or no control over the prices they can charge or the level of quality they must deliver – all of this is determined, often spontaneously, by the "big boys," the giants in logistics and shipping, petrochemicals, pharmaceuticals, electronics, insurance, finance, and banking. The owners of small and medium enterprises are often as bewildered and powerless as the people they employ.

Prices nowadays are often not set by any conventional measure of competition. Multinational companies can set prices as if they are monopolies irrespective of whether they are the only player in the market or not. Then the tendency of networked information to be generated socially, and circulate freely, undermines the capacity of capitalists to stabilize or retain ownership of intellectual property. The violation of copyright laws is rife as the general public routinely share pictures, movies, and music, without regard to who actually owns them.

To be sure, giant monopolies – Google, Amazon, Spotify, Facebook, Twitter, and the rest – have disrupted the nostrum that "supply and demand" determines prices. Indeed, not only are prices arbitrarily fixed, the relative scarcity of information goods – texts, music, formulas, and sequences – has to be maintained, in defiance of their evident "natural" abundance, by monopoly proprietors. They go to court, or employ technological fixes, that attempt to limit the choices of their customers, but there are always ways around. The customers themselves promote free access by the "theft" of intellectual property. They simply disregard copyright and find ways around the smart technical barriers put in place by the big capitalists.[19]

What is more, the proliferation of free goods seems to defy all conventions of commerce. For example, email is free. Before the proliferation of email people incurred considerable postal and telephone charges. Now, although the costs of a computer or smartphone, and the necessary internet connection, are considerable, the free stuff available, hour-by-hour, day-by-day, outstrips the "entrance" costs by some considerable degree. Our free stuff is paid for by the take up of paid-for add-ons, by the sale of our personal information to advertisers and promoters, and by advertising thrown up on the free services we access.

Free this, free that, and free the other is an astounding and confusing aspect of modern capitalism, because, of course, nothing is free in commercial society. Everything is, in one way or another, paid for handsomely so that the multinational corporations can remain in business. All this lies some way beyond the capacity of most proprietors and business men and women, as much as it does the people they employ. Commercial society is, like a hall of mirrors, capable of endlessly confusing appearances. To the worker, the employers appear to be and are all-powerful, while most business people think of the consumer as king. On the other hand, big business thinks in terms of market share and interest rates, controlling what they can and cannot do. One is reminded of the rhyme of Jonathan Swift, rewritten by Augustus De Morgan:

Greater fleas have little fleas upon their backs to bite 'em,
And little fleas have lesser fleas, and so on ad infinitum.

And the great fleas themselves in turn have greater fleas to go on;
While these again have greater still, and greater still, and so on.

Nobody appears to be in charge. In fact, nobody is actually at the wheel as we career along in an increasingly dynamic society in which technical innovation and commercial competition appear to be unraveling everything as we go.

Although this seems to be an entirely new situation, it is not. It was Karl Marx who noted more than 170 years ago that:

> The bourgeoisie cannot exist without constantly revolutionising the instruments of production, and thereby the relations of production, and with them the whole relations of society. Conservation of the old modes of production in unaltered form, was, on the contrary, the first condition of existence for all earlier industrial classes. Constant revolutionising of production, uninterrupted disturbance of all social conditions, everlasting uncertainty and agitation distinguish the bourgeois epoch from all earlier ones. All fixed, fast-frozen relations, with their train of ancient and venerable prejudices and opinions, are swept away, all new-formed ones become antiquated before they can ossify. All that is solid melts into air, all that is holy is profaned, and man is at last compelled to face with sober senses his real conditions of life, and his relations with his kind.[20]

As Eric Hobsbawm noted: "Marx and Engels did not describe the world as it had already been transformed by capitalism in 1848; they predicted how it was logically destined to be transformed by it."[21] They were certainly wrong in the *Communist Manifesto* about the simplification of the class division between the workers, and the owners of capital, but we can all now see how right they were about the dynamic nature of commercial society. Competition, technical innovation, and the changes in culture and the modes of life that arise spontaneously, inevitably affect us all, and add to the perplexity we often experience when we attempt to grasp the nature of the world in which we all live.

Chapter 2

Class Confusions

Class is a perplexing notion in the kind of commercial society in which we live. It is the source of considerable anxiety and much speculation. It is present in different forms in different places, and has a special texture and resonance in England. Here there is a great to-and-fro between a person's "objective" class position, and their "subjective" understanding of their own place within the "class" set-up. There is a kind of parlor game in which people award themselves and others their appropriate place on the scale of an imaginary "class system," as if classes were real crowds of people, competing for their place, grasping at the rungs of a social or cultural ladder.

In commercial society, classes are simultaneously real and unreal. Now you see them, now you don't. Distinctions of class are painfully obvious to anybody who wants to take a stroll through any city. The life chances and opportunities of the people one passes on any walk, moving from one neighborhood to the next, are startlingly different. Deeply ingrained disadvantage and privilege are plain to see on every side. We do not need the skills of an anthropologist, the qualifications of a sociologist, or of a cultural critic, to see what is blatantly obvious. Yet these sharp differences seem to blur and blunt the closer one looks for some more profound, or stable, mode of distinction.

There are no classes when we are children. Everybody we know exists without sociological position. To the extent that we become aware of differences between people, they do not, and cannot, assume the status of categories, because we have yet to learn how to organize and rank differences in an orderly manner. Yet I was aware of important social differences from a very young age. My mum had been hired as a maid-of-all-work for a wealthy doctor, when in 1928 she arrived in London from Cashel in the Irish Free State. Intelligent, gregarious, and resolutely optimistic, she had been poorly educated by nuns, and was always held in the embrace of menial work.

When I was growing up in the early fifties, she was a cleaner in the houses of very rich people in London's St John's Wood, and in mansions up in Hampstead. She regaled us with stories of the lives these people led, and often came back with foods which were exotic to us, like cream cheese, black bread, rollmops, sauerkraut, olive oil, and garlic. Both my parents had worked in posh restaurants in London's West End, so they were familiar with a great many things that were strange and usually unobtainable to people "in our walk of life," as mum would put it. I don't remember anything about "class," though, apart from "classy," of course. The manifold differences in wealth and culture did not automatically translate into an articulate account of class awareness, although as kids of 9 or 10 we always stoned the cars of Tory candidates at election times, and used peashooters on the big black police cars that swept through our streets.

These childhood impressions about class culled from the middle of the last century were intrinsically confusing, and rarely coalesced into a definite shape. I suspect the vagaries they revealed continue to this day. They are governed more by markers associated with cultural consumption – food eaten, movies watched, clothes worn, neighborhoods lived in – than anything more theoretical. Taste in furnishings, pictures, and music, all orchestrated by our personal demeanor, accent, and way of speaking, sense of humor, table manners, and much else.

There is not even agreement that class differences actually exist; some people argue that we live in a "classless society" or in one in which we all belong to the same class described, according to personal taste, as "the working class" because most of us have to work, or as "the middle class" because most of us aspire to the state of grace encompassed by the phrase "middle-class values."[1] We also have those people described as pond life, underclass, the posh, wealthy celebs, and a mass of sub-categories, including rural toffs, various urban tribes, and everybody from those whose only way is Essex, or made in Chelsea, to classy bohemians, grungy squatters, and the ragged sleeping in doorways. It is a shifting cast of characters and classifications that changes in a kaleidoscopic manner around the perennial labels of working, middle, upper middle, and upper class.

By the time I was 18 or 19, in the mid-sixties, I had become acutely class conscious. Thinking about this reminds of me of Quentin Crisp, who once said of a working-class lover, "He'd fallen on the thorns of class, and bled." Of course, I didn't bleed; I was a card-carrying communist, and an active trade unionist. I was also elected by my union branch to the trades' council in Leeds. Trades councils were delegate bodies composed of representatives from the branches of different unions in a particular town or city. In Leeds, the trades council was composed of around 60 or 70 delegates and we met monthly to discuss matters of common concern in the old trades' hall on Fountain Street. I remember a white-tiled bar, it was like drinking in a public lavatory. Our gatherings were distinctly proletarian with a large contingent of communists, organized by Bert Ramelson[2] to intervene in an organized way in the discussion and votes taken at the meetings.

So far so good. However, I was a window dresser at the time. I spent my working days artfully placing shoes, gowns, gorgeous fabrics, furs, and wildly expensive handbags, made from snake and crocodile skins, in shop windows. All objects Wen Zhenheng would have described without hesitation as "superfluous things."[3] Well, my trade union brothers – they were all brothers – and my party comrades took the view that participation in luxurious activities was deeply suspect, and seriously doubted whether I was a member of the working class at all. I think I got away with it, as far as I did, because I was young and callow. But it was made clear to me that "working class" meant those who worked with their hands in factories or toiled at backbreaking labor, that did not really include titivating silks and satins ruched into sumptuous tumbles in department store windows.

On one occasion I got into very hot water indeed. During a vote about a May Day demonstration I voted in support of a proposition put up by a member of the Socialist Labour League, a notoriously Trotskyist organization, resolutely opposed to Soviet reality, and the Communist Party of Great Britain. This was a serious mistake and I was duly hauled over the coals at a meeting in the Communist Party rooms in the market buildings on New York Street. I remember this as a pretty alarming experience as a 19-year-old, facing a room full of men made hard by lives of hard labor, and tough times during the fighting in Spain, Italy, and France. My "mistake" in voting with a Trotskyist was apparently hard to forgive. I had only one ally in the room, a doctor, a Jewish comrade who'd fled from Vienna in 1938. He managed to defuse the situation, despite his class credentials being as suspect as mine. However, it didn't save me from a private encounter with Bert Ramelson in his office. With a bust of Lenin on his desk, Bert was quietly threatening. "You seem rather a nervous person, Don," he noted. I'm not sure to this day what relevance this remark had to my voting the "wrong" way, but I was clearly a suspect of some kind to a man well-versed in the art of interrogation, and detecting lapses in political rectitude and class loyalty.

I now know that my class problem arose because of the dynamic and fluid character of capitalist society in which long-standing assumptions and realities are dismayed and disrupted by changes beyond anybody's control. The parents of the older staff in the department store where I worked had, in the thirties and forties, paid the company a premium in order to secure a place for their 14-year-old kids in such a grand establishment. These workers, eventually promoted to buyers and heads of department, felt they had acquired the good taste and breeding of our wealthy customers, by long familiarity with polite society, and extremely well made and expensive goods. In some mysterious way the superior character and manner of our customers had rubbed off on them. They had obviously come to feel that, simply by working in the realm of luxury with furriers, milliners, livered doormen, and a calligrapher who wrote all the price tags by hand, they had acquired a superior social status derived from their place in the store. These snobbish shop workers were as dismayed as those in the trades council by what was beginning to happen in the prematurely named, "Swinging Sixties."

One must remember that this was almost a decade before *Ziggy Stardust* and that lightning bolt across Bowie's face, and 15 more years before Margaret Thatcher began to unravel Arthur Scargill's world.

Yet as early as 1956 the ground had begun moving under everyone's feet. In the context of the botched invasion of Egypt, known as the "Suez Crisis," the old oligarchy that had run the country for the best part of a century was beginning to feel the mismatch between its well-honed attitudes, accents, and assumptions, and the emergence of a society in which deference was declining while diversity was increasing. [4]

In fact, the celebrated values of colonial discipline and honor, conspicuous courage for King and Country in the face of the "natives," had been lampooned for years. *Colonel Blimp,* the irascible, jingoistic old soldier created by cartoonist David Low in the mid-thirties, was a caricature of excessive military virtue and imperial prejudice, whose days were numbered as early as 1934; not even the Second World War saved his bacon. By the premiership of Harold Macmillan, 1957-1963, and particularly the "Winds of Change" speech, delivered by "Super-Mac" in Cape Town in February 1960, the writing was on the wall for the *Pax Britannica*. This was the speech in which the prime minister publicly signaled the end of Britain's colonial empire; decolonization, which had been an integral component of state policy since the independence of Ghana in 1957, was now openly on the agenda; the colonies were beginning to slip away in a mess of bad faith, bloodshed, and misplaced optimism.[5]

Super-Mac was the creation of the cartoonist *Vicky* (Victor Weisz). This image of Macmillan stuck. In 1958 Stephen Potter had published *Supermanship, or, how to continue to stay on top without actually falling apart*; it's a satirical look at the cultural reality of Britain at the time.[6] The title was strikingly apt as Britain became accustomed to "the orderly management of decline" in everything from its failure to stop Colonel Nasser's nationalization of the Suez Canal, to the headlong decay of our textile and engineering industries.[7] In the face of this Harold Macmillan greeted the electorate in 1959 with the observation, you've never had it so good:

> Indeed, let us be frank about it – most of our people have never had it so good.
>
> Go around the country, go to the industrial towns, go to the farms and you will see a state of prosperity such as we have never had in my lifetime – nor indeed in the history of this country.[8]

He wasn't lying, or exaggerating. The old oligarchy was facing enormous shifts in public attitudes to life and power, no doubt brought on by unparalleled prosperity. Things were still tough for most people, but they had never been better; with full employment and rising wages, change on every front was in the air. Like the advance or retreat of Greenland's glaciers, older ideas of the stability of class divisions began to dissolve gradually, and by the late fifties were melting into notions of a society given over to ideas of choice and style.

The avalanche of white goods and televisions pouring into working-class homes by 1960 dismayed many socialist intellectuals. They could see only the trickery and blandishments of advertisers in the rising prosperity. New suites of furniture bought on payment plans were announcing the mismatch between reality and their ideas about class. The leading cultural critic at the time, Raymond Williams, denounced advertising as magic. He thought advertising was:

> ...a highly organized and professional system of magical inducements and satisfactions, functionally very similar to magical systems in simpler societies, but rather strangely coexistent with a highly developed scientific technology.

Most workers did not regard televisions, washing machines, possession of a wristwatch, sachets of shampoo or instant coffee, and the chance of an annual holiday away from home as "magical inducements and satisfactions," but on the contrary as real improvements in their lives. However, the belief widespread among the working class at the time, that advertised goods could satisfy real needs, was understood as an expression of "false consciousness" by leftist critics. Williams insisted that:

> If the meanings and values generally operative in the society give no answers to, no means of negotiating, problems of death, loneliness, frustration, the need for identity and respect, then the magical system must come, mixing its charms and expedients with reality in easily available forms, and binding the weakness to the condition which has created it.[9]

Lying behind these sentiments was the belief that the common-sharing and community that many socialists regarded as emblematic of working-class life was being undermined by the individualistic aspirations that seemed to be arising spontaneously with the new prosperity. Even Stuart Hall, who, along with Raymond Williams and Richard Hoggart, was a leading cultural critic, was disturbed by the impact of increased spending power on the outlook of working-class people.[10]

Mass consumption seemed to be trumping the virtues of homogeneity and social solidarity that many socialists associated with the working class. However, the supposed value of "sameness," and fear of diversity was being steadily undermined, not only by rising prosperity, but also by large-scale immigration from the Caribbean, Pakistan, and India. The old certainties thought to typify the white working class were to prove unsustainable as the texture and composition of working-class life was beginning to change beyond all recognition.

The arrival of large numbers of people of color from a wide variety of different ethnicities and social and economic circumstances through the fifties and sixties of the last century threw a boulder into the lake of class assumptions. Many people came from vastly different rural settings from each other, in the Caribbean or in Pakistan and India, others came as refugees from East Africa, with the experience of running their own businesses and enterprises. All initially entered the traditional jobs and neighborhoods of the white working class. Many arrived penniless or at least in very straightened circumstances, but worked like Trojans as manual workers on low pay, fighting their way into the lower echelons of the middle class, by buying shops, food outlets, and other small businesses. The class experience of many immigrants had few parallels among Britain's white workers, whose experience of entrepreneurship and individualistic enterprise was extremely limited.

More recently, immigration from Europe, China, Turkey, Nigeria, and many other places has complicated things still further as a plethora of Turkish barbershops, Polish delicatessens, and Vietnamese nail bars have proliferated in working-class neighborhoods and markets. The Labour Party's assumption that the disadvantages and discrimination often suffered by these newcomers would make them natural Labour Party voters has begun to whither, and the broad left's belief that people of color would simply join the white working class in some simple or uncomplicated manner has been grievously disappointed. These changes had thrown a spanner into the works, and posed a radical threat to notions of class common in Britain until the early sixties, when disruptions of ideas of position, rank, and hierarchy were crowding in from all sides.

I was 18 in 1963, and before moving to Leeds, I was working in the accounts department of a firm in Southwark, South London. The building where I worked had an elevator, but its use was restricted to senior staff. Consequently, people like me, a lowly clerk, were not allowed to ride in the elevator. This, of course, was a "red rag to a bull" for a bolshie kid like me. So, almost from day one, I would ride up with the superior folk to the accounts department. Nobody ever said a word, except I was eventually taken to one side by the chief clerk and warned about my shameless defiance of the rules. Despite this, nothing was done, and I was not sanctioned or dismissed. Clearly, the company's managers knew themselves that the game was up. Petty status distinctions could no longer be defended or tolerated.

This was beginning to occur with people's accents and ways of speaking too. During the early forties the BBC had to hire Wilfred Pickles, who had excellent diction, but a Yorkshire accent, to read the news. This departure from John Reith's strictures[11] was prompted by the BBC's need to distinguish between themselves and the public-school accent of William Joyce's fascist broadcasts from Berlin. Joyce's way of speaking was routinely lampooned by the BBC in dubbing him "Lord Haw-Haw," a strange moment for an institution committed to the perpetuation of the dulcet tones and haw-haws of the British upper class.

This public-school accent[12] and figures of speech are perhaps best exemplified by Celia Johnson and Trevor Howard's modes of speech in Noel Coward's 1945 movie *Brief Encounter*. Interestingly, the speech of the working-class characters, played by Stanley Holloway and Joyce Carey, are deployed for comic effect. This is particularly the case with Joyce, who plays "Mytle Baggot," the lady who runs the station buffet with amusing "airs and graces"; Myrtle displays her social refinement and spurious superiority with a vulgar accent fashioned especially to sound like an imitation of a properly posh, if strangled, person.

However, BBC announcers and those giving wireless talks continued well into the sixties, using the accents and figures of speech learned at public school, known as received pronunciation. With the emergence of public figures like The Beatles, Michael Caine, Twiggy, and others from the lower orders, even the class distinctions associated with accents and ways of speaking began to break down. The markers of social class were being undermined by a new spirit of choice and diversity born of mass consumption, and the break-up of old elites as new social elements began to achieve wealth and prominence in society.

These shifts toward greater choice regarding the way one might live started to drive a coach and horses through the traditional notions of class position. Mass motoring, and even home ownership, came steadily into view. Things were made even more confusing when flights abroad, traditionally the preserve of the well-to-do, began to become commonplace as the package-holiday classes poured into General Francisco Franco's Spain to escape Britain's dismal licensing laws, and worse weather.

So it was that rising living standards, mass consumption, and lifestyle choices freed up millions from the straight and narrow prohibitions of yesteryear – which was not really the dim or distant past – but merely a few years previously, when the birth of commercial television broke the BBC's broadcasting monopoly in Britain in the autumn of 1955, and *Super-Mac* entered Downing Street a couple of years later; the same year that some grandees of the Church of England came out in favor of ending criminal sanctions against homosexuals.[13]

Despite the long hangover of licensing laws dating from the First World War, and the closure of more or less everything on Sundays at the behest of Lord's Day Observance campaigners, alongside those of the Union of Shop, Distributive and Allied Workers (USDAW), the publication of *Lady Chatterley's Lover* signaled the end of an era. D. H. Lawrence's erotic novel of love between a high-born lady and a gamekeeper had been banned since 1928, yet after 9 days of trial at the Old Bailey on November 2, 1960, it was found not to be obscene. Prosecutor Mervyn Griffith-Jones revealed the absurdity of the *ancien régime* with his famously anachronistic question: is this the kind of book "you would wish your wife or servants to read?" A year later the take-home pay of ordinary industrial workers was beginning to catch up with professional footballers' *maximum wage* of £20 a week.[14] So following the intervention of the Trade Union Congress and the threat of a players' strike, the *maximum* was hurriedly scrapped, opening the doors to untold riches as formerly working-class soccer players secured their share of revenues from television broadcasts of football matches.

Nobody was in any doubt that radical changes were afoot.

This was the context in which class began to be seen by many as a matter of choice. This dismayed many people leading even John Lennon, in support of Raymond Williams's thesis, to insist that "they":

Keep you doped with religion and sex and TV
And you think you're so clever and classless and free
But you're still fucking peasants as far as I can see
Working Class Hero, Plastic Ono Band, 1970

Most working people, of course, did not take such a dismal view of their situation as the millionaire musician and the well-heeled cultural critic. Many clearly believed that, freed from the class hierarchies of yesteryear, they could aspire to be anything they liked.

Strict Marxists, of course, continued to insist that class was nothing to do with consumption, choice, or lifestyle. These things were more or less irrelevant. Class was determined by one's relationship to the means of production, and nothing else.

Those who owned capital – wealth used to employ people to make profits – were "bourgeois" or "capitalists"; those who had to work for wages for employers were working class. As simple as that.

Well, Marx and Engels had to retreat from the simplicities of the *Communist Manifesto* of 1848 pretty rapidly, as it became clear that the growth in the size and complexity of industry complicated rather than simplified the class structure. By the end of the nineteenth century, there were many differences and divisions arising from variations of skill, income, and cultural attitudes among workers which, together with the expansion of employment in retail, and a raft of "white-collar" technical and administrative occupations, complicated class relations in entirely novel ways. The idea that classes were composed of undifferentiated masses of people, with an unmediated "relation to the means of production," was certainly not sustainable from any cultural or political point of view.

This has deleterious effects on the thesis that social change occurs as a consequence of class struggle. It is not at all clear that the great social and economic struggles that have occurred throughout the life of commercial society, and even before its emergence, can be described as "class struggles." All recorded important political and industrial battles in the past have involved a bewildering mixture of people, aspirations, and occupations (or only a fragment of a particular class), however you want to figure it. There are no examples of revolutions, social struggles, strikes, and upheavals that can be said, strictly speaking, to have been class struggles. The great revolution in France found aristocrats, and court officials, on both sides. In the English revolution of the seventeenth century, substantial landowners, agricultural laborers, and religious dissidents of one kind or another were well-represented in the opposing armies of the English Civil War.[15]

This process of admixture, coalition, and the bewildering variety involved in social and political strife continues to this day. Class is never a decisive or determining factor in profound social upheavals. This truth presents an important theoretical challenge to Marxists, and many others on the left, for whom it is axiomatic that "class struggle" is the motor of historical change.

This has led to the situation in which the left, who have traditionally seen society in terms of class, resolutely committed to determining the "objective" class nature and content of particular struggles. It gives rise to a kind of mythological approach in which struggles are shoe-horned into one's theoretical constructions, regardless of the perplexing nature of reality. Movements are said to be objectively bourgeois or working class regardless of their actual social composition because the class nature of particular struggles is determined not by sociological means, but by the objective nature and purpose of the aims contested.

Clearly there are political demands raised by working people that are decisively working class in their origin and appeal, the Ten-Hour Movement of the 1840s, and the battles for male suffrage in the 1860s are important examples. The demand for more social and council housing also springs readily to mind. All demands for intervention by the state in the provision of affordable housing, for both purchase and rent, have a distinctly proletarian motivation and flavor. However, there are vast cross-class struggles like those against the Poll Tax, 1989-93, the fuel protests when farmers and truckers blockaded oil refineries in autumn 2000, or more recently, when a huge coalition was formed against the government of Boris Johnson over the Covid-19 examination debacle of 2020; what is striking in these struggles is the overwhelming element of class unity between working-class people, great swathes of the middle class, and some sections of the business community.

Unsurprisingly this throws up considerable confusion, given that much of the population continues to view their class position subjectively, and, even when people accept the categories popularized by the socialist left, insist on being both working class and recalcitrantly Tory. Of course, it was well-known by figures as diverse as Karl Marx, Vladimir Lenin, and Oscar Wilde[16] that one's objective class position cannot be relied upon to result in the political outlook that theories of objective class interests would dictate.

Tony Blair, a year before his first general election victory, set the cat among the pigeons in the 1996 Labour Party Conference at Blackpool by instructing delegates to:

> Forget the past. No more bosses versus workers. You are on the same side. The same team. Britain united. And we will win.
> https://www.youtube.com/watch?v=-oDB667TB18

This, of course, was nonsense then, and it is nonsense now. It's the kind of thing that only a millionaire politician could say and expect to be believed. We all occupy radically different positions in the class structure and while it is perfectly true that the interests of employees may often coincide with those of their employers, they do not in some generally applicable sense share the same interests, worries, or concerns. On the contrary, the decisions of employers, taken *exclusively* on behalf of shareholders (as they are required by law to do), often impact very badly indeed upon their employees.

In a country like England, and in Britain generally, there are also intractable class divisions expressed in the education system where schools and universities are broadly ranked on the basis of their material, scholarly, and intellectual resources. It goes without saying that the children of those with substantial amounts of capital, those of parents in positions of prominence and leadership in the professions and state institutions, go to the best schools and universities. At school, the privileged attend classes of no more than ten and often fewer; at university they enjoy one-to-one tuition or very small group seminars. As a matter of course, these young people are encouraged to work harder and develop greater skills of self-organization and discipline in the context of institutions that make greater and more measured intellectual demands upon teachers and students alike.

By contrast the children of the mass of working people have access most readily to schools and universities of much poorer quality in terms of material resources and of the ratio of teachers to students. So it's pot-luck for most kids; this mass provision is of variable quality, ranging from the excellent to the truly appalling.

The class distinctions and prejudices, which spontaneously arise as a consequence of these divisions, together with objective differences in the resulting skills and abilities possessed by the young people sieved through this educational colander, often stay with them for life. They are made worse by the suggestion that the glittering prizes awarded to those who attend the best schools and universities are in some way merited because they are naturally more intelligent and deserving than those who go to ordinary schools and inferior universities, or indeed to no universities of any kind. This is, in fact, the most pernicious aspect of class relations, in modern or liberal democratic capitalist societies, where inherited family advantages and inherited wealth are routinely camouflaged as being the result simply of "merit" and "meritocratic" systems of assessment.

Of course, many people of modest means continue to make their way into the professions and even into the capitalist class, despite the numerous obstacles which stand in their way. However, this does not mean that class and class distinctions are irrelevant any more than the election of Barack Obama to the presidency could be taken to mean that Black or Hispanic people, or the children of poor white parents, would no longer face enormous obstacles blocking their entrance into the professions or into the managerial and employing ranks of society.

So class continues to matter a great deal; it continues to shape the life chances of many millions of people in the wealthy capitalist countries. Perhaps the easiest way of understanding the class structure is to think about the nature of a person's occupation, as much as their income, and as much as their ownership of capital. The working class can be thought of most usefully as all those people who do routine manual or clerical labor – people who have little or no say in the tempo or the organization of their day's work. The middle class consequently can best be thought of as those people who have more control, responsibility, and input, into the structure of their working day and/or the terms of their employment; middle-class people have a large measure of control over how they perform their jobs and may have access to professional organizations and institutions capable of controlling or supervising entrance to their profession.[17]

Consequently there are huge variations *within* classes and *between* classes, just as there are enormous numbers of tiny capitalists with only one or two employees, who in some abstract sense can be said to occupy the same class position as those employing tens of thousands of workers. The truth is that class relations in commercial society represent a large shifting social terrain in which people simultaneously occupy many different and contradictory positions. For example, millions of workers own capital in the form of savings in building societies, banks, and pension funds. Some workers may even have bought a second house or flat, which they rent out to tenants.[18] Some capitalists own very little capital and have had to put up their family's house as collateral against their bank loans. Indeed, in the "private sector" your boss is most likely to be a small capitalist with fewer than 20 or 30 employees with whom you have personal contact on a daily basis. In the "public" sector your supervisors or managers are likely to be drawn from a range of different professional groups, or may simply be drawn, by promotion and competitive staff development routes, from the general labor force.

It will be readily seen from all this that modern capitalist society cannot in any strategic, political, or economic sense be understood as the product of class struggle. Conflicts most certainly exist between people who are differently situated within the hierarchy of income, education, occupation, and power. But it is not at all clear that these conflicts can be said to coalesce around the classes defined in communist, socialist, or anarchist rhetoric as the "working class" or the "capitalist class" or the "middle class," or even around the similar categories which have emerged from traditional forms of Marxist theory. It is true that Marxists have often designated particular social movements as "objectively" "working class," or "objectively" reactionary, as a way of dismissing the importance or relevance of their actual social composition in order to achieve "a better fit" between their theoretical constructions and the world itself.

Some modern Marxists like Antonio Negri and Michael Hardt have attempted to conceive of the aggregate of working people as a more diffuse social formation to which they have given the name "multitude".[19] By this means they clearly hope to elude the historical limitations of the "working class" as earlier Marxist thinkers and militants have conceived it. But this move is not quite as radical a shift as it seems at first sight as Antonio Negri demonstrated by insisting that the "multitude" is simply the modern form or instantiation of the working class.[20] The grounds for this theoretical move to the "multitude" remain important, however, as a way of incorporating many different elements of the productive population from women working in the home, to those engaged in new occupations and activities like software and website designers, who might appear to have no cognates in the older Marxist conceptions of the class structure.

Despite these conceptual maneuvers, social conflicts have not, throughout the history of capitalist society, ever corresponded in any overwhelming or decisive sense to class lines or class loyalties, determined by "the relationship to the means of production" of those involved. Great social movements and upheavals have always been composed of a complicated admixture of different classes and social forces or only of fragments or sections of particular classes with a sprinkling of support from other classes.[21]

Despite the rich iconography of class struggle on the left, and exhaustive historical accounts of strikes, riots, insurrections, and communes, and of the counter measures taken by soldiers, magistrates, and police, often involving hard-fought battles, and armed conflict between "classes," there is little evidence that the forces marshaled in such conflicts were actually "class" forces; when looked at more closely, one is constantly struck by the sectional character of the social elements involved. By and large, throughout the history of commercial society, the defense of private property, whether in the form of capital or consumption goods, forms the keystone in the arch of bourgeois or capitalist society, and unites most people, irrespective of their class position, around a range of fundamental commitments to the bourgeois state and capitalist relations. The conflicts between demands for more social insurance, or for more freedom for private capital do not have a class character; they divide all social classes and sections within classes to a greater or lesser degree.

One can only conclude that classes continue to exist, and that one's class position might often have a determining influence on the course of one's life, but that classes do not seem to possess any decisive relevance in the political life or direction of wealthy capitalist societies. They form an important constitutive part of everybody's social experience, and inform many of our social assumptions and personal calculations, but they do not permit us to articulate any general demands or express any wider loyalty or class commitments beyond the level of the nostalgic mythologies associated with historical reflections on the left, or with our own biographies.

Chapter 3

Who's Exploiting Who?

Exploitation is not the word most people resort to when confronted by a lousy job, a rotten boss, or being paid peanuts. Where there is a burning sense of injustice, it is usually inflamed by indignation at the way we are treated. Of course, we know the company makes a profit – if it didn't, we wouldn't have a job. We know too that the people who own the firm are richer, often much richer than us. They've got better cars, and live in smashing big houses or sleek apartments. This is because the world is not fair, and "money goes to money" rather than to those who need it. Inequality is a given, ordinary, universal reality, as far as most of us are concerned. We certainly don't need to be told about it by socialists or lefties banging on about "exploitation." We already know that the firms we work for, the factories, offices, shops, workshops, or bureaucracies, would be nothing without us. No money would be made without us, and without the boss making money we'd all be out of work. We know in practice, full-well, how commercial society works.

I once worked for a training firm in Stockport. It was a private company although at least 80 percent of its business and income came from the government in return for the training we offered to unemployed youths. There was a lot of running up and down stairs to the photocopier, lots of preparation of workbooks designed to improve the lads' computer skills, English, and CVs. The job was OK and the pay was reasonable. However, it became obvious to the proprietor and managers that a number of my students were making fraudulent travel claims – getting money that they were not entitled to. This was very small beer in the scheme of things, but the boss took the matter very seriously indeed. The poverty of our students was no concern of hers. The upshot was that I was responsible because they were my students. Although I had no role in the theft, it was thought that I must have turned a blind eye to the fraud. I was arraigned in front of the proprietor and an array of managers, and found guilty as charged. I was not sacked, but I swiftly found another job, in a rage of indignation at the injustice of it all.

I jumped from the frying pan into the fire, because the firm I went to, owned and managed by observant Muslims, thought it was perfectly reasonable that my colleagues made it known that they thought I shouldn't be employed there because I was homosexual.

In every job I've ever had – messenger, clerk, warehouseman, window dresser, cleaner, kitchen porter, builder's laborer, papermill maintenance, shelf stacker, administrator, typesetter, further education teacher, and finally a university lecturer – my own problems and difficulties have always mirrored those of my workmates and colleagues. In every place I've ever worked the unhappiness of workers revolved around the way they were treated. The unfairness of managers in promoting one person rather than another, the ludicrous character of the demands made by supervisors, and the absurdity or irrationality of changes in work routines, clearly produced by people who knew bugger all about the job in hand. Not being respected, not being consulted, not being valued; in my experience these have been the principal causes of misery at work. Nobody has ever mentioned exploitation.

It is true that I have never worked in a sweatshop. And if I had, whether it was in the rag trade in Leicester or Mumbai I suspect my bitterness would be focused rather more on piece-rates, wretched take-home pay, long hours, dodgy electrics, overcrowded workrooms, and the danger of poorly maintained machines. The difficulty of arranging childcare and getting time off to look after sick relatives without losing one's job would loom large. Then there would always be the abiding fear that if one complained too much, the boss could always replace you at the snap of his fingers. I suspect the unfairness of it all, the brutal irresponsibility of the employer, the bullying of overlookers, or sexual harassment by supervisors, all these would crowd in on you, without any need for a theory of exploitation.

There is clearly a need for active local trade union organization, but often the informal power of one's colleagues can be enough to rectify a wrong. I remember an amusing occasion when I was sent by the labor exchange to work on a building site. I was appalled by the idea, so I went to the site, wandered around, and then went back to the exchange with the tale that I couldn't find the site foreman. In the event, I was sent right back, and the foreman set me on a job clearing impacted rubble with pick, shovel, and wheelbarrow. A couple of days later, I was ordered down into a large hole to clear a pipe junction of mud and debris. "But it's full of water!" I expostulated. There was soon a little crowd gathered around the hole, around me, and the foreman. The skilled men, bricklayers, plumbers, electricians, were hugely amused by my horror at having to go down into the watery depths. "The lad's right," they all chorused, "You'll have to get a pump and pump the water out before he can go down there." They knew I was an entirely incompetent novice laborer, and thought it was a hoot, to get one over on the foremen. So I was the beneficiary of their malicious delight.

Working people have many ways of dealing with bullies and other injustices in the workplace, from trade unionism to the informal exercise of their influence with colleagues to offset that of the managers or supervisors. It can work in many different ways; I remember an occasion when I was a manager, having to deal with the problem of a worker who was simply incapable of turning up on time. She was always late, and not very good at her job, but I was aware that if I attempted to sack her, I would reveal my own incompetence as a manager. The upshot was, I simply put up with her tardiness until I was promoted to another role in another office. On a previous occasion, in a different organization, I recommended an irretrievably lazy person for promotion as the only way of getting rid of her. And so, it went on...exploitation doesn't ever seem to have been an issue.

In general, the popular use of the word exploitation means merely taking unreasonable advantage of someone. Consequently, it has many and varied uses. It can be applied to situations in which people have very poor wages or very bad working conditions. The word is often applied to employers or supervisors, who insist upon making demands of employees or subordinates, which are regarded as generally unreasonable by those on the receiving end. Exploitation can even be applied to interpersonal relations in circumstances where a friend or partner uses their social, emotional, or erotic power to control or manipulate those around them. And it seems to be universally applied to those who are very poor anywhere in the world; they are routinely referred to as being exploited irrespective of their actual circumstances or of their relationship to employers or landlords.

In the Marxist tradition, however, the word exploitation has a much more precise meaning. When applied to pre-capitalist relations it simply means the extraction of surplus wealth from the direct producers over and above basic food, clothing, and shelter. So peasants or slaves were exploited because any surplus wealth, which they produced in the form of crops, textiles, or other manufactured articles, was directly appropriated or seized by their landlords, masters, or owners. Exploitation, in this pre-capitalist sense,[1] was understood in a fairly simple and direct manner regardless of the form it assumed. Of course, God, or gods, of one kind of another, invariably ratified a ruler's authority, and that of his princes and satraps, and their underlings. Complex hierarchies of obligation and obedience tied ruler and ruled together into the kind of social relationships in which wealth was taken from the laborers and artisans and given to the "high born." Whether this wealth was seized in the form of rent, taxes, tithes, or fines, in money or goods, it was the confiscation of the surplus produce, whatever that was, by the rulers, whoever they were.

When Marxists discuss *capitalist exploitation* the theoretical focus shifts from the extraction of surplus wealth in this relatively direct sense to the more complicated idea of "surplus value." Under capitalism, Marxists argue, exploitation takes the form of the expropriation of "surplus value." Surplus value is produced when workers make commodities whose value is greater than their costs of production – including the wages of those who made them.

For example, in the course of a day the worker makes 100 cameras, and is paid £125 in wages. The other costs involved in making 100 cameras, including materials, machinery, equipment, buildings, rent, and shipping, amount to £11,550. So costs, plus labor, amount to £11,675 for the production of the 100. The cameras are then successfully sold for £136.99 each. So the capitalist receives £13,699 in return for the cameras. From this sum he must deduct the costs of producing the next 100 cameras, leaving him with £2,024, from which he must pay £467.50 in interest on his loans, and save £856 for research and development, advertising and promotion; this leaves him with a handsome return of 6 percent (or £700.50) on his original investment for himself and his shareholders, if he has any.

This final sum left over after the profits have been divided between replacement and reinvestment, interest, research, and promotion – this £700.50 – is the surplus value. For the Marxist it is the extraction of this surplus value from the labor of the worker which constitutes exploitation. For Marxists exploitation exists when surplus value is being produced by workers and appropriated by their employers. This is because, according to Marxist theory, this surplus value is produced by labor; it is not produced by the raw materials, or by the ingenuity, organizational skills, or the risk-taking initiatives of the employer; it is entirely produced by the worker who was paid £125 for their day's labor, which has in turn produced an extra or "surplus value" to the tune of £700.50 which is then legally appropriated by the capitalist, because the capitalist owned (or had borrowed) the initial outlay of £11,675.

It is important to remember that according to this theory, it does not matter whether the good or commodity being produced is a camera, a computer program, a massage, a dry-cleaned suit, or the performance of a singer. The surplus value is produced in a similar manner whether it is a physical commodity or an apparently immaterial service. As long as the people who are paid wages by a private employer are producing the good, a surplus value will be produced by the worker and will then be appropriated by the employer. If something goes wrong and profits are not gained from the sale of the good, a competitor will either swallow the firm, or the company will simply go out of business.

According to this view the capitalist who mobilizes the resources needed to make products, and provide services, makes no contribution to the profits and values produced. This runs counter to the experience of entrepreneurs, and those who bring investors together to fund new ventures, who evidently believe that they make a big contribution to the foundation of businesses which, in the fulness of time, declare profits and pay dividends to their shareholders. However, most socialists and communists are grievously ignorant about business and money-making. This is why they argue that entrepreneurial activity is merely a technical function that could be carried out by employees, and there is no reason at all why the investors should have control of the surplus value produced by the workers.

Despite the strength of this opinion, it is difficult to conceive of circumstances in which commerce could flourish without the ingenuity, flair, and preparedness to take risks, which define those who start-up and develop businesses of all kinds. True, many capitalists are simply "time servers," quietly running established companies, with little energy or ingenuity. However, it is problematic to argue that the capitalist, whether go-getting and inspirational, or dull and pedestrian, does not play a large and active part in the creation of surplus value generated by any successful company. Business acumen, knowledge, and initiative with regard to the market, and accurately anticipating the demand for entirely novel products, must also rank as ingenuity in the estimation of the contribution which capitalists make to the vital role of workers in both manufacturing and developing goods and services which sell well.

In sharp contrast, it is vital for those who want to sustain the idea of exploitation to believe that the capitalist makes no meaningful contribution to the production of profits; it is essential to those who want to argue that the surplus value appropriated by the employer is the source, or expression, of the exploitation of labor by capital. Exploitation is, according to this view, said to reside in the fact that the business owner takes full control of all the profits, and decides how and in what proportion they are divided up between everybody who has a claim on them. He can do this because he has raised the loans and privately owns, outright, the funds used to finance production. The worker, on the other hand, has already been paid a wage for their time, skill, and energy, and because s/he does not contract the loans or raise the capital, has no claim on the profits.

So one can readily see that the fact and reality of exploitation is not merely contested, it is more or less independent of the level of wages or the quality of working conditions. A very highly paid and very skilled worker who works in excellent conditions of safety and security may well be producing much more surplus value, and hence be much more exploited, than a person on lousy wages who works in rotten and dangerous conditions.

There is another problem, and this is the theoretical distinction that some Marxists argue exists between "productive" and "unproductive" labor. In this theory "productive" labor is labor that produces "surplus value." Labor that does not produce "surplus value" is said to be "unproductive labor." Consequently, the work of nurses and porters in the UK's National Health Service or in any other state-run service is not productive because it does not produce surplus value. This explains, the proponents of this theory would argue, why the private capitalists are always eager to keep the costs of these necessary, but unproductive, activities as low as possible. Spending on activities which do not produce surplus value is only justified from the point of view of the capitalist if it can be demonstrated as essential for maintaining a social and economic environment that is favorable for making profits and generating surplus value. This is what capitalists mean when they say we must concentrate on "wealth creation" rather than wasting money on bureaucracy or too many teachers or too much on other public expenditures.

So this narrow conception of the Marxist theory of exploitation also suggests that the work of women in the home as mothers and carers, of charity workers, and the many and varied activities of the unemployed or those who are simply not employed because of disability or age is also unproductive, because none of this enormous amount of labor – which certainly exceeds in hours and energy that which is carried out for money wages – produces surplus value. Therefore, the labor of the majority of the population is said to be unproductive; consequently, the majority of the population are not, strictly speaking, exploited at all.

Marxist theorists and political activists overcome this

difficulty by arguing that exploitation can only be thought of and calculated at the level of the whole economy; exploitation can only be understood as an expression of the class relations as a whole. In making this move, contemporary theorists are following closely upon Marx's own practice of moving from the "concrete" to the "abstract." He was closely concerned about the way that workers contributed by their labor to the creation and re-creation of the plant, machinery, and buildings with which they work. This takes place within a particular branch of industry, and extends to "the total social capital" of a country.[2]

As a consequence, the exploitation of the worker in the capitalist enterprise is expressive of the exploitation of the entire working class, whether they are engaged in productive or in unproductive labor.

It is at this stage that the Marxist theory of exploitation appears to lose much of its precision because in the face of the actual presentation of class relations where great masses of working-class people produce no surplus value at all, it becomes vital to move the discussion onto a much more abstract level where it is necessary to talk about the working class "as a whole" being exploited rather than any particular individual, or any well-defined groups of individuals within the working class. This is often approached through discussion of the contributions made toward the production of surplus value from beyond paid employment by, for example, women's unpaid work in the home.[3]

It should be remembered that this is not a recent problem. The tendency of Marxists in the past to concentrate their particular efforts upon the organization of male industrial workers was not because these workers were considered to be more productive of surplus value or more exploited. For most Marxist and communist activists, the attraction of male industrial workers lay in their strategic importance in power generation, transport, and exports. Winning support among workers concentrated in these sectors would confer much greater strategic and tactical power and influence in any struggle with the capitalists and their state than organization among more dispersed and diffuse sections of the working class.

So despite arguments to the contrary, the factories, the docks, the road transport fleets, the railways, the power stations, the steelworks, the coal mines were of particular or special interest to these activists because workers in these sectors were always able, through strike action, to bring the capitalist economy to a grinding halt, and in the right conditions were always thought able to provoke political crises, which were regarded by agitators as providing great opportunities for the advance of communist or socialist politics and the development of a radical consciousness throughout society. Although some theorists tried to argue that the "factory" is important because it was *the* site of exploitation, *the* site of the production of surplus value,[4] in reality the importance of manufacturing and heavy industry to the revolutionary was its strategic value for trade union and leftist militancy.

Therefore, the difference between modern radical communist theorists like Michael Hardt and Antonio Negri and more traditional Marxist accounts of exploitation are not as great as some would argue. Whereas Hardt and Negri argue that exploitation takes place at the level of the "metropolis," which is the site where the exploitation of the "multitude" takes place, the traditionalists say that exploitation takes place at the level of the entire working class. Traditional Marxists have to say this because when pushed to show how a nurse working for the NHS, a garbage collector or fire fighter working for the state or a local council is exploited they have to talk more abstractly about class relations, because according to the strict account produced by their theory, these state employees are unproductive of surplus value and consequently are not exploited at all, whereas a waged hairdresser, for example, is indeed exploited by the owner of the salon. This kind of emphasis would, of course, be politically unacceptable to all concerned, so it follows that they must, like Hardt and Negri, suggest that exploitation takes place at the level of the "multitude" or of "the working class," whichever concept and term you prefer.

What emerges are a number of sharp differences between Hardt and Negri's kind of account about what is needed to mobilize large numbers of people in struggle against commercial society, and the more traditionalist accounts concerning the working class. The differences are not, in truth, about exploitation. On the one side the traditionalists want to emphasize the need for a focus upon the organization of waged workers in their workplaces, on the other side are those who follow the more contemporary or mainstream anti-capitalist position, who want to emphasize the need to focus at the level of the entire community of working people who produce the common goods and common values, which are then, in a variety of different ways, appropriated by the capitalists through the processes of commodification and privatization. So the more modern anti-capitalists think that exploitation takes place at the level of the community, known as the "multitude," and attempt to work across the networks which compose the "metropolis" in order to subvert and undermine the commercial system, while the traditional Marxists want to continue to talk in terms of class and of organizing working-class resistance in the workplace in order to overthrow capitalism.

Neither the traditional Marxist account, nor the more modern Hardt and Negri account of exploitation is satisfactory. We are still left with the problem of how to determine precisely who it is that produces the growing wealth of capitalist society and who it is that appropriates it.

Clearly, if somebody comes along and simply takes something that you have made in your own time, with your own resources, they are stealing from you, regardless of the legal explanations that might be deployed to justify the confiscation – it would be exploitation of a most direct kind. But this is not what happens in commercial society, except when criminals steal from us.[5] A capitalist is somebody who mobilizes sufficient funds in order to be able to employ people (to pay them wages) to make things in anticipation of gaining a profit once what has been made is sold. A thief, on the other hand, is a person who steals something that doesn't belong to them. We may rhetorically call storeowners, bankers, and employers in general "robbers" and "thieves," but in truth we all know the difference between a criminal and a capitalist.

Of course, it remains axiomatic for all anti-capitalists that it is the workers or the multitude who produce the wealth, and the capitalists who appropriate it, but none of the available anti-capitalist accounts appear to be able to show beyond the level of generalities who is exploited, and by whom.

There is no doubt that many people simply believe that glaring social inequalities in relation to income and hours worked are sufficient evidence of exploitation; they do not need a complicated theory. The evidence of "their own eyes" reveals the injustice at the heart of the capitalist system.

However, these manifest inequalities exist throughout the entire population. We do not live in a society in which the plutocrats live at one end and everybody else lives at the other. Society is composed of a mass of different people living in a great spread of different circumstances and incomes. And however you want to define the "working class" or "the multitude," there is no way you can avoid the great variety of differing levels of wealth and power which exist *within* the working class, or *within* the multitude.

If we suggest that exploitation is simply revealed by inequality then we would be compelled to conclude that exploitative relations exist *between* poorer workers and better-off ones; *between* supervisors and line-managers, and the people they manage; *between* workers living in rich countries and those living in poor countries; exploitation would indeed become so diffuse a concept that it does not seem to me that it would be a very useful idea at all.

However, this is precisely the point of view of many contemporary anti-capitalists, extinction rebels, social justice warriors, and the "woke" in general. They are transfixed by the horrifying levels of inequality in the world in which not much more than 2 billion have acceptable standards of living while the remaining 5.8 billion live somewhere between perpetual insecurity, severe poverty, or actual starvation. This leads many contemporary anti-capitalists to conclude that we live so well *because* so many are starving; they believe that those of us in the rich countries are well off because we exploit the masses of people who live in the poor countries, through the benefits we derive from cheap imported clothing, food, and other materials.

This extremely widespread point of view suggests that exploitation arises from the *prices* paid for consumption goods rather than within the manufacturing process itself. Consequently, many people believe that if we simply paid more for certain goods this could be translated into higher wages, and consequently, there would be less exploitation.

From these options, taken together or individually, it will be seen how inadequate the various notions of exploitation available to anti-capitalists actually are. Evidently, those who express an active hatred of commercial society have not yet produced a robust or general theory of exploitation. Consequently, they cannot identify the exploiters and the exploitative relations with the degree of clarity that would be needed for the elaboration of a general solution to the problem, or be persuasive enough to win the support of an overwhelming body of public opinion. This is why, I suspect, it is justice and fighting injustice *not* exploitation that motivates most anti-capitalist, ecological, or woke campaigns. It is the tangle of relationships between ideas of justice and injustice, between equality and inequality, which dominate these movements rather than Marxist ideas of class, multitude, or exploitation.

Chapter 4

Surviving Inequality

Inequality in life appears to be baked-in to the human condition. I remember when I was a university teacher observing that a fair proportion of my students were more intelligent than me – maybe as many as half of them. More intelligent? What could I mean? I mean that they could think quicker, had better memories, were articulate without the *ums* and *ahs* to which I am prey. These advantages were evidently a function of their youth as much as anything else, but we were certainly not equal. I knew more than these young people, and could put ideas and evidence together with greater assurance than them, but this cohort was, in a performative sense, certainly more intelligent and able than me. This is unsurprising and unexceptional.

The same might be said about good looks and attractiveness. Some people are more beautiful than others, and some young women and men can, unaccountably, charm the birds out of the trees, regardless of their beauty, or lack of it. I have often pondered on the unfairness of it all, to no avail.

I remember sitting in a pub in Oxford in the company of a crowd of extremely posh Baccalaureate students from all over Europe. They were around 17 or 18 years old, and their confidence as they laughed and joked in three or four languages, moving easily from one to the other, was truly astonishing. Not only that, they were exceptionally well groomed and tanned, with flawless skin, they wore their clothes in a manner worthy of *Vogue, Flare,* or *Dazed.* It was enough to make an ordinary person spit feathers with envy. These gilded young people were quite obviously the beneficiaries of inherited advantage.

Wealthy parents can ensure that their offspring get the best of everything, and go to university at Oxford, Cambridge, or Yale – maybe only to the London School of Economics, Imperial College, or Rutgers. The advantages enjoyed by their kids are in some sense undeserved, but in another, their graduations are the glittering prizes won by those who've worked very hard, and been shredded through the mill of grueling examinations. The result of this inequality is, by and large, that they are more able and more competent than those who've lacked their built-in advantages. They write and speak with greater fluency, know two or three languages well, and have a smattering of several others. They have an easy familiarity with "high" culture, and are equally at home with the popular music, movies, and fads of their time.

This is all radically unfair. It mirrors the truly horrifying levels of inequality of life throughout commercial society, both within the wealthy countries, and between them, and with the very poorest places of the world where the truly wretched of the Earth struggle for food, clean water, clothing, and shelter, day-by-day. Many people on the left lay this dreadful situation firmly at the door of the capitalists. Commercial society is, they imply, uniquely vicious, uncaring, and unequal. I can certainly see why they do. When I step out of my upscale apartment block in the middle of Manchester, I am confronted by ragged people begging in doorways and the careworn bustling off buses with their kids and buggies from the poorer parts of the town. I need only walk for 20 or 30 minutes in any direction from where I live to find myself in another world, where life is often eked out from week to week, and month to month, in insecurity on miserable pay, and worse welfare checks.

However, I am not at all sure this glaring inequality is really the fault of the capitalists. Perhaps Christ was right when he said:

> For ye have the poor always with you; but me ye have not always.
>
> Matthew 26:11, King James Bible, 1611

This fabled saying of Christ is more of an observation than a prediction, but you can see what the authors of the *New Testament* were driving at in the 50 or 60 years after the supposed date of the Crucifixion, or indeed the translators of the seventeenth century. Inequality and poverty were endemic as far as they were concerned, and they had good reasons for thinking so. Throughout recorded history there have been ruled and rulers, rich and poor. Great and wealthy merchants, satraps, princes, kings, and pharaohs, together with artisans, peasants, masses of slaves, paupers, and lepers. So far as we can tell there has never been equality anywhere, at any time. Even in societies that have not generated urban life or state power in any form, the manifest differences between men and women, young and old, and what might be called the natural aptitudes or skills of individuals, appear to have always militated against equality.

What is historically peculiar about capitalist society is that since the emergence of commerce as the determining activity, the abundance of goods of all kinds has been growing to a degree unparalleled in all previous ages. The mass of goods produced and commercially traded in Holland and England began to increase exponentially from the latter decades of the seventeenth century. This deluge of stuff has increased more or less year-on-year ever since. Commercial society and the innovations it prompted in agriculture, navigation, mining, manufactures, and machine production has created vast wealth, enabling the creation of sewerage systems, unparalleled improvements in communications, medical science, education, transport, and healthcare. It has resulted in societies in Western Europe, North America, Australasia, Japan, and South Korea of stupendous wealth. Yet the central paradox of capitalism is that this vast increase in the wealth of society has not resulted in the abolition of poverty or of gross inequality.

Very large numbers of people have been lifted out of absolute poverty in China over the last 30 years, and conditions for those at the bottom of the heap have been steadily improving. In Britain, by and large, the poor have waterproof shoes, phones, warm clothing, indoor plumbing, baths, showers, and double glazing. Yet in 2020, 1.6 million people used foodbanks in Britain, and a third of those – well over half a million hungry people – were dependent on handouts because of delays in welfare payments. Those without a roof over their head have an even more dangerous, miserable, and bewildering time of it, lingering on the streets, in the midst of plenty. Because the paradox remains, commercial society – the civilization determined by buying and selling everything from food grains to human labor power – has proved itself to be utterly incapable of distributing its mountainous bounty in any manner that approaches equality or justice. Inequality and unfairness appear to be baked-in to the life of commercial society in a similar way to that of ancient empires, feudalism, or absolute monarchies.

Before the end of the eighteenth century, everything from food, textiles, footwear, and housing was literally in short supply. Then, when plagues and sunless summers befell us, famine came calling. There really was not enough to go around, some people – those at the bottom of the heap – had simply to starve quietly to death, nothing could be done for them. With the onset of the nineteenth century, with the vast increase in commerce and the growth of machine production, this ceased to be true. Since then, famine and murderous poverty have been produced by war or failed social policies, never by an actual shortage of foodstuffs. From the catastrophic failure of the food supply in Ireland in 1848-1849, to the Bengal famine of 1943, or the Biblical scenes of starvation in Ethiopia in 1983-1985, or of Yemen in 2020, famine was not the result of absolute shortages, but of the disastrous effect of political choices made by national governments and international agencies. Even the Soviet, or "communist famines," the Holodomor in Ukraine in 1932-1933, China's Great Leap Forward of 1958-1962, and North Korea's "March of Suffering," 1997, were not produced by natural or unavoidable shortages, but by the pursuit of the state's priorities by those in power, in rank opposition to the interests of the population in general.

The protests of anti-capitalists and the outrage of social justice warriors is produced by this bitter paradox – a land of milk and honey in which billions are denied a place at the table. There is no doubt, no doubt at all, that there is enough of everything to go around. We really do have the technical capacity adequately to feed, clothe, and house everybody on the planet. Yet the whys and wherefores of commerce, market relations, and political arrangements appear to prevent fair shares for all.

This thought prompts a memory of seeing the movie *Elysium*, released in 2013. In this film the Earth has become a planet of slums and the wealthy have retreated to a large and wonderful space station, visible from Earth, in which the rich and powerful live lives of ease and plenty. A dismal flight of fancy you might think, except that not long after seeing it, I was traveling, first class, to the Far East in an Airbus A380. Here I traveled in luxury, with the best of everything, and even took a shower in a fully equipped bathroom, at 40,000 feet. While I was lathering with creamy soap, refugees were drowning in the Mediterranean, and the lands over which we were flying were parched for the lack of clean water. It struck me then that the movie *Elysium* is no more than a ham-fisted metaphor for the world we actually live in.

The brutal inequality in which we all live is enough to drive any decent person into a frenzy of outrage. This is why the left – the anti-capitalists, the social justice warriors, the woke – are keen to be "on the right side of history." Convinced of their own virtue, the left-liberals, the socialists, and the anarchists spare no effort and leave no stone unturned, in the struggle to put distance between themselves and the wickedness of capitalist society. They fail, of course. Over the years when handsome fountain pens and leather-bound notebooks gave way to Filofaxes and slim silver ballpoints, and these in turn were replaced by smartphones, laptops, noise-cancelling headphones, and AirPods, the mightily active dissidents of the urban uptown world, those on the lower decks of *Elysium*, have never for one moment limited their personal consumption to what they imagine is necessary for the good life. A tiny minority gripped by ancient mysticisms, or thoroughly modern survivalist conceptions, keep chickens and goats, power their houses with sustainable technologies, and live entirely off the grid. These options are, in yet another bitter paradox, available only to the privileged few – which is why most anti-capitalists find themselves stuck, inescapably, in the all-consuming maw of commerce.

Those who hate commercial civilization, the capitalists, and all their works – the broad left in society – find themselves gripped by the politics of virtuous guilt. They never stop banging on about those less fortunate than themselves, they never cease from talking about the appalling circumstances of those at the bottom of the heap – the homeless, those on welfare, the manifestly disadvantaged of all kinds. It is as if fixation upon the fate of those who've fallen under the wheels of the commercial juggernaut will serve as atonement for the sin of not being among the fallen and the destitute. It is much more than "virtue signaling"; it is a deeply ingrained response to the guilt felt by the relatively well off at not sharing the fate of the poor, feckless, and disorganized, who often find themselves in extremely straightened circumstances.

Critical race theories come from a similar school of thought, finding themselves unable to do anything much about the disadvantages that many people of color the world over have experienced, and in some measure continue to experience; they have opted to "decolonize the curriculum." Such people assure us that it'd be much better if white people shut up, and accepted that simply being white makes them racist. This is because, regardless of the real history of white serfs, peasants, laborers, and workers, regardless of their actual circumstances in the here and now, white people are all the beneficiaries of the historic oppression of black people. This thought provides a welcome opportunity for the expiation of all the advantages white people are said to have gained from historic crimes, which modern white individuals have not actually committed. White people find that they are expected to wander in this moral, historical, and philosophical maze, berating themselves for iniquities they had no part in.[1]

This kind of thinking, and the politics it leads to, does nothing to address the problem of inequality at all. As the rapper Akala frequently notes: "Unfortunately, the world is not fair."

However, Akala's succinct observation, as he well knows, doesn't carry the full story, because on its own, it does not deal with the question of intention. Is inequality – the maintenance of inequality – intentional? Is it deliberately selected by the powers that be in commercial society? Do the rich and powerful strive to enshrine inequality in society? The answer to these questions is *yes*, and *no*. Faced with problems that they think are inherently insoluble, the powers that be will always tend toward ensuring that they, and theirs, are given the best chance in the miasma of inequality in which we all find ourselves. Hence, lavish private schools (called "public schools" in England), expensive first-class medical care, elite universities, and so it goes on. Faced with inequality, which they can do nothing about, the wealthy are predisposed to make the best of things in circumstances which are not of their choosing.

Now the leftist response to this reality is to suggest that

inequality is directly created and sustained by the "ruling class" and the capitalists, by the very measures that the wealthy employ to ensure that they and their kids get the best of everything in a world (which as far as the wealthy are concerned) is irretrievably unfair and unequal, has always been so, and always will be. "Why should we send our kids to inferior schools when we can pay for the best?" "Why should we use public hospitals when our insurance will cover the best private medical care available?" "Why should we fly coach when we can afford first class?" The wealthy ask these questions because they do not believe that "A better world is possible." They do not believe equality is possible or even desirable, given the catastrophes that have followed in the wake of all previous attempts to achieve equity by turning the world upside down.

Now the difficulty here is that most of the poorer people in society, the working class and the lower middle class, broadly share a similar outlook with the wealthy. They do not think that in our wicked *fallen world*, equality is ever possible. They know that if they could afford it, if their lottery numbers came up, or they found the *crock of gold* at the end of the rainbow, they'd make damn sure that they and their kids got the best of everything. They are well acquainted with the hypocrisy of well-heeled leftist politicians who denounce selective education, but send their own children to very expensive fee-paying schools.[2] They are well aware of well-to-do leftists who denounce tenants for opting to buy, at a discount, the council house (project homes) or apartment they've lived in for years, while buying grand houses and apartments for themselves in the private sector that most people could only dream of.

The principal socialist response to this reality is to retreat into a mythological realm. During the late nineteenth century many wealthy socialists looked back to the radical priests and revolutionary peasants of the fourteenth century.

> *When Adam delved and Eve span*
> *Who was then the gentleman?*

> From the beginning all men by nature were created alike, and our bondage or servitude came in by the unjust oppression of naughty men. For if God would have had any bondmen from the beginning, he would have appointed who should be bond, and who free. And therefore, I exhort you to consider that now the time is come, appointed to us by God, in which ye may (if ye will) cast off the yoke of bondage, and recover liberty.

These are said to be the words of John Ball, a Lollard priest from Colchester. Little is known about him, and much that is, is produced by the gentlemen he was attacking. Provenance to one side, John Ball was asserting that by nature we are all equal in the sight of the Lord, and should therefore all be equal in society. This, essentially mythological account, beloved by socialists from the nineteenth century onwards, is that the Original Sin was not eating the forbidden fruit from the Tree of Knowledge in the Garden of Eden, nor even Cain's murder of his brother, but the introduction of inequality into the world by the "gentry."[3]

So according to this account, inequality is the intentional product of the wealthy, who hold their wealth against the rest of us in order to not only become wealthy in the first place, but to use it to maintain their place at the top of the society's pile. Socialists hope that by perpetuating the resentment of the poor against the rich they can increase their chances of winning over the population at large to their side. The truth is, of course, that the poor need no encouragement to resent the wealthy; this arises spontaneously, and does not need revolutionary newspapers or websites to enhance or proliferate resentment. In what is often called "the politics of envy," the less fortunate quite naturally wish they had it better, and that they too could get a slice of the easy prosperity enjoyed by the well-to-do. But, much to the perennial dismay of socialists over the years, this popular resentment does not lead working people effortlessly toward believing that inequality is the invention of the rich. This socialist fantasy is not shared by the mass of the population. They know that inequality is baked-in and cannot, except in the *Dream of John Ball* or *News from Nowhere*, or *The Sermon on the Mount*, be wished away.[4]

Oh, it's the meek! Blessed are the meek! Oh, that's nice, isn't it? I'm glad they're getting something, 'cause they have a hell of a time.
Mrs Big Nose, *Monty Python's Life of Brian*, 1979

Although most of the population in Britain are not actively Christian in any sense, they do know that Christ is said to have been on the side of the poor, and that, apparently, he was an advocate for the disadvantaged. This is the mythological realm in which people often see socialist aspirations as a nice idea, a lovely dream, that cannot possibly come to pass. In this respect, ordinary working people find themselves in lock-step with the wealthy. Only the revolutionary socialists and anarchists stumble along a different path.

Most left-wingers fight ruthlessly against the inevitable, by attempting to depict their opponents as uniquely vicious, immoral, and wicked. In this vein, Tories, and conservatives in general, are said to be utterly uncaring about the fate of those less fortunate – the low paid, the disabled, and the oppressed. The fact that conservatives simply see many social problems as intrinsically insoluble, and believe that they should do everything they can to ensure that as many people get jobs as possible, as being the only way of mitigating the negative effects of life in commercial society is utterly disregarded by most socialists. "No!" they insist, "Tories are bastards and liars!" – committed only to profit and the pursuit of self-interest. This leftist misunderstanding is, of course, fueled by widespread *in-work* poverty, and by egregious examples of Tory perfidy and conservative heartlessness, but at root it has its origins in the idea that the prosperity of the well-to-do lies at the heart of our problems.

This radical confusion can be seen in the protests of people against so-called gentrification of former industrial districts along canals or rivers, that, before containerization, housed docks and warehouses. Something similar is happening in city centers where disused commercial buildings are being renovated as residential lofts, or replaced by upscale apartment blocks. In London and other cities, older neighborhoods, that were for a time resolutely working-class areas, find that rising house prices and rising rental yields turn what was formerly a low-rent area into a high-rent one, with all the accoutrements – the restaurants, coffee shops, and delicatessens – required by the better-off newcomers. The response of many socialists to these developments is to blame the people who move into these new flats and rebuilt neighborhoods. The young professionals can pay higher rents because they have better jobs, or can share the rent with partners or friends; consequently they are often denounced as the new "gentry." It is implied by many on the left that those fortunate enough to be able to move into these desirable properties are somehow responsible for the disadvantage suffered by poorer people, who may find themselves priced out of the area. The brutal inequality of society is then laid at the door of the man or women usually in their late twenties (or thirty-somethings), because they're lucky enough to earn £35,000 a year rather than £18,000.

In this way, the traditional instinct of the radical left, and of socialists in general, to blame the better-off for the condition of the poor is sustained even when it leads to the absurdity of denouncing upper working class and lower middle-class youngsters, as if they are the bourgeoisie, responsible for all the ills of the world because they are well-paid. The well-to-do on the left hang on to their credibility by ensuring that they always remain on the 'right side of history'; mouthing at every opportunity their deep concern for the poor and oppressed wherever they can be found. This is always the occasion where the social justice warriors, the woke, and the anti-capitalists often reveal their ignorance of history by eliding the difference between civil equality on the one hand and social equality on the other.

The famous slogan "Liberté, Égalité, Fraternité" expresses sentiments associated with the great French Revolution of 1789, as if the revolution was really about brotherhood, equality, and liberty.[5] The truth is, however, the vast revolutionary upheaval, which embroiled all sections of French society in struggle, actually had little or nothing to do with social equality. Despite the prominent participation and demands of laboring men and women, and of the slaves in the "French" Caribbean, the revolutionary deputies in Paris had little to say about social conditions. All women, all slaves, and most men were incapable of "active citizenship." Indeed, after the promulgation of the *Declaration of the Rights of Man and the Citizen* in 1789 just over 85 percent of the population were denied the vote; they were incapable of participating fully in the political affairs of the republic. It is true that the Convention in 1794 abolished slavery. But 8 years later, First Consul Napoleon Bonaparte restored human bondage. This reversal was short-lived, however, because a year later French troops had been thoroughly thrashed by the revolutionary slaves of Saint-Domingue,[6] and all French claims to territory in North America were surrendered to the United States.[7]

The 17 articles of the *Declaration* make clear that what was sought was civil equality for men of property in France freed from the arbitrary corruption of royal or noble authority. Wealthy men had before the revolution been prevented from equal access to the state, official jobs, pensions, and contracts by aristocratic privilege. The revolution put an end to that with Articles I to XVII of the *Declaration*. Property was to be protected but the social rights of the poor and disenfranchised were beneath notice. The provisions relating to the presumption of innocence, against arbitrary arrest, imprisonment, torture, and those articles that widened the right to trial, freedom of speech and conscience were of interest to all, but abolition of social or material inequality was not stated or intended.

In our day, too, we can all understand the limited idea of "equality before the law," and of equal civil rights with regard to access to jobs, housing, education, and the provision of public goods, like healthcare, access to hotels, restaurants, and other publicly offered services. However, socialists and the radical left are often guilty of a lazy elision between these civil rights with regard to the state and legal equality, on the one hand, and equality of income or condition on the other. The fantastical aspiration and demand for the abolition of material inequality is poorly if ever thought out by revolutionary socialists, anti-capitalists, social justice warriors, or the woke in general. Yet they continue to ignore the undoubted fact that the general view among working people is that a world without inequality is simply a day-dream, dreamed only by thoroughly impractical persons, or a dangerous ambition by people destined to impose some ersatz notion of equality upon us all by force.[8]

So it is that despite manifest confusions, the idea that inequality is caused by the capitalists, or the wealthy in general, is not widespread. Most working people understand that given half a chance we would all take advantage of the opportunity to rise in the world, and benefit rather more from what is unequally available than we do at the moment. Socialist rhetoric concerning *greed* is certainly popular, and belief that *greed* lies at the root of all inequality is extremely common. However, this thought that *greed* is a cardinal sin, and a real problem, sits quite easily alongside the widely shared ambition among working people to do better in the world – earn more money, get a better, or more interesting job, live in a nicer neighborhood, have good clothes, and marvelous vacations. In this sense the accusation of *greed* is pitched at those who are popularly believed to have *too much of everything already*, whereas *our* ordinary aspirations for a better life are entirely reasonable.

When I was a young man in the 1960s the thesis of *embourgeoisement* was much discussed in the sociology departments of universities and colleges. It addressed the, often bewildering, changes that were beginning to take place regarding the cultural and social identification of white-collar workers with the middle class. Thinking about this many years later I was amused when I realized that my journey from the working class into the middle class started in the Young Communist League. The YCL, which I joined at 15, and the Communist Party of Great Britain, which I joined at 18, was in a sense my grammar school or sixth form. Having left a secondary modern school to work full-time at 15, my education continued in the YCL where we learned about different kinds of music, were encouraged to read books, and discuss things, which in the normal course of our lives we would never have encountered. From Bessie Smith and Leadbelly, to Mozart's *Cosi fan tutte*, and Beethoven's Fifth Symphony, from Mandate Palestine to Israel, from Bertolt Brecht to Arnold Wesker, from the *Iliad* to the Peasants' Revolt of 1381; we also learned of Sisyphus' hubris, and of Prometheus' courage in stealing fire from the gods. It was in the YCL that the world began to open up. Through this, together with a broader culture of self-improvement through correspondence courses and night classes, one strived to improve one's grasp of what was going on, and simultaneously to improve one's situation by getting a job as a clerk, while aspiring to be what my dad, always called "a schoolmaster," which was evidently the ceiling of his ambition for me, beyond which he could not see.

The paradox here is amusing – a political life committed to the advance of working-class interests – coupled with an aspiration to do everything one could to leave the narrow confines of working-class life as far behind as possible. The abiding desire was to be able to get a job that gave you a wider measure of control over your day and how you performed your work – to leave behind the world of routine manual or clerical labor for good. I am quite sure that I was not alone in harboring these contradictory thoughts. Even today, I see the left of the Labour Party, Labour councils, many trade unions, and the do-gooding "voluntary sector" stuffed full with working-class youngsters striving to better themselves. At least half of the upper echelon of the working class in the UK strive to get into universities or gold-standard apprenticeships, in the hope of doing well enough to escape the boredom and low pay on offer in rather more humdrum jobs.

Persecution you must fear
Win or lose you got to get your share
You've got your mind set on a dream
You can get it though hard it may seem now

You can get it if you really want
You can get it if you really want
You can get it if you really want
But you must try, try and try, try and try
You'll succeed at last

I know it, listen

Rome was not built in a day
Opposition will come your way

But the hotter the battle, you see
Is the sweeter the victory now

You can get it if you really want
You can get it if you really want
You can get it if you really want
But you must try, try...
Jimmy Cliff, 1970

Of course, Jimmy Cliff knew, along with most of his audience, that success is not guaranteed, "but you must try, try and try, try and try..." This is how most working people cope with inequality, by steadfastly trying to improve their situation, by gambling, buying lottery tickets, taking dance or singing lessons, learning to play musical instruments, making music in their bedrooms, learning to "code," going to "uni," enrolling on Open University courses, gaining new skills, and getting promoted. Sadly, for those of us stranded in the grip of socialist or communist ideas, this paradox in wanting to emancipate the working class, while striving "manfully" to leave it behind, continues to exert a powerful attraction. Most working people find themselves entranced by the culture of commercial society, unable to extricate themselves, practically or imaginatively, from the substantial blandishments on offer by life inside the inequality we all embrace.

Chapter 5

Entranced and Bewildered

I am constantly dazzled by the culture of commercial society, by its plenitude, its multifarious forms, and its startling ambition. It's no wonder that most of us binge on boxsets, follow the floor arrows obediently around IKEA, and max out our credit cards for unmissable bargains on flights, transfers, and hotels, in places with palm trees, and marvelous beaches. Kids go free! Older ones, and young adults, spend much of their time fighting to defend *All Reality* in their bedrooms on *Fortnite*, while others are spending 30 pounds (or 45 dollars) they don't have battling in America's Wild West in *Red Dead Redemption*!

People are often gripped as much by social media as by gaming, and if you're anything like me, it'll be wall-to-wall drama on television. Before the emergence of commercial society most laboring people saw very little drama, perhaps a religious play once a year in the market square or played out on a rostrum in the church porch. In modern conditions we see a drama perhaps every day, and sometimes several plays a day. These might be full-length movies, episodes of a favorite series, or a regular "soap." There is a vast industry pumping out comedies, tragedies, revenge tragedies, and as Raymond Williams, pompous as ever, pointed out in the 1950s, "an obsession with criminal delinquency." We do love crime fiction, along with historical romances, sci-fi, and seriously scary movies. They "take us out of ourselves." I can remember my mum telling me "to suspend disbelief" at our weekly trip to the pictures. She didn't use that phrase, of course. She simply told me when I was 12 or 13 that I needed "to lose myself" in the picture. This is what she always did, whether it was a film or a romantic paperback, set in improbable circumstances. She loved stories, she was always transported to the far beyond, by tales which took place in exotic circumstances, at the ends of the Earth.

When you step back a bit, and consider the rich density of our culture, the experience of commercial society, which envelops us, wraps around us, the entire world, and everything we do, it is truly astonishing. One has to ask: How did we get here?

One morning in February 1625 the Portuguese merchant ship *Nossa Senhora da Guia*, crossing from Manila to Macao, was wrecked on the rocks of an isolated stretch of the Chinese coast. As the survivors struggled ashore, the Chinese villagers and local officials were astonished and threatened by the variety of races, strange languages, and peculiar clothes of those rescued from the waves. Although the ship was Portuguese, the majority of the passengers were from "literally everywhere on the globe." They were from Luzon, Mexico, Brazil, the Canary Islands, Germany, and Holland. "Europeans may have dominated the sea-lanes of the seventeenth century, but Europeans were only ever in a minority on board."[1] Portuguese and Dutch traders were traversing the globe buying and selling as they went. In the process they spontaneously commenced the intermingling of wildly different cultures, peoples, and races.

Commercial society is unique in the history of the world in being truly global. We know that North Africans lived in Vindolanda, just south of Hadrian's Wall in Northumberland, England, during the fourth century AD. There were Persians, Greeks, and Jews from Palestine in Rome at the same time, but nobody from Java, Peru, India, China, or Japan. It was the growth in international trade in porcelain, spices, silks, and other exotic goods that started to bring rural and communal isolation to an end; it must have been like aliens landing from outer space for the Chinese peasants encountering the survivors from the shipwreck of the *Guia*. These rural laboring people had no connection at all with people of different races from foreign lands, and no experience of the ship's cargo, because it was stuffed full of unimaginable luxuries, luxuries for the rich that were beginning to open up the world we live in today. As Wen Zhenheng might have noted, it was trade in "superfluous things" that spurred on the merchants of the Dutch East India Company to risk all in their struggle to succeed.[2]

When Hernán Cortés entered the Aztec Empire in what's now Mexico in 1519, there were no horses in the Americas, no apples, bananas, lemons, oranges, onions, coffee, rice, or wheat. In Europe in the sixteenth century, there were no chilies, tomatoes, potatoes, rubber, cacao, or tobacco. The conquest of the Americas, initially by the Spanish and Portuguese, and then by the inroads made by the Dutch, the English, and the French in the seventeenth century brought together many of the plants, roots, and fruits from both Europe and Asia to the Americas, introducing new food crops from the Old World into the New, changing the cuisine of peoples from India to Italy, from Ireland to Virginia.

Consequently, the culture of commercial society was from the seventeenth century composed of an unparalleled conjunction of different influences from across the globe. Of course, the strange societies that Europeans encountered across the world were not isolated from each other. The Japanese knew a lot about China, and the different peoples and cultures of what is now Mexico knew a lot about each other, and so on, across the world. People with different habits, food, clothing, and spiritual beliefs have always been influenced by those from neighboring places. As Claude Levi-Strauss suggested in his article "Race and History":

> We should not, therefore, be tempted to a piece-meal study of the diversity of human cultures, for that diversity depends less on the isolation of the various groups than on the relations between them.[3]

It is clear that relations between different peoples from different cultures have always been important – merchants from Amsterdam, Delft, Den Haag, or Lisboa did not suddenly increase contact between peoples in particular regions of Asia, or the Americas. For example, the people of Java had always known a lot about the different folk in Sumatra and those from what is now Malaysia, but it was European merchants who introduced peoples who had never had much contact between each other on different continents, separated by vast oceans. The effect and impact of the seamen and traders from the North was, for the first time, truly global.

It was to the commerce between Europe and the rest of the world in luxury goods that the culture of capitalism owes its origins. With bitter irony in 1972, Randy Newman sang:

And every city the whole world round
Will just be another American town
Oh, how peaceful it will be
We'll set everybody free
You'll wear a Japanese kimono
And there'll be Italian shoes for me
Randy Newman, Political Science, 1972

In this typically leftist take on things, Randy Newman was attributing most of the world's troubles to big rich countries like America (or Britain in the past). Such places are to this day often accused of gobbling up everything and dominating the world with their own things – McDonaldization, Starbucks, the Kardashians – with their goods, their music, their styles, and their inventions.[4] Like modern America, such powerful places have often been said to overwhelm everyone, everywhere, and everything with their own culture. The truth is, however, that the culture of commercial society, the culture in which we all live, is a bit different from that, because as Claude Levi-

Strauss argued, cultures very rarely develop in isolation, but by constantly reacting and absorbing influences from their neighbors. This truth has particular importance for us, because our "neighbors" are global, and our culture has been developing globally, and becoming more and more so, since the middle of the seventeenth century, with every decade that passes. It is also true that in recent years the universal access, particularly to music from all over, has not only resulted in a new vibrancy, but also carries with it the danger of homogenizing or of the flattening of cultural expression.

The reason that many English people used to rate calico very highly, wear pajamas, live in bungalows, like Chicken Tikka Masala, and love brown sauce made with dates, spices, and tamarind has got a lot to do with the British conquest and occupation of India. The fact that educated Indians all speak English and many love cricket, Jane Austen, and much else that comes from the cultures of the British Isles has a similar cause. The close relationship between England and British possessions in India had far reaching effects. Following the great rebellion in 1857 these lands became the British Raj, which was consolidated in May 1876 when Queen Victoria was proclaimed Empress of India.

Ferdinand Maximilian Joseph Maria was an Austrian archduke and a younger brother of Franz Josef I, Emperor of Austria. Between 1856 and 1860 Ferdinand Maximilian had a palace, built on the Adriatic at Trieste. It's called *Miramare*, and has a garden clearly designed in anticipation of Paradise. Four years after *Miramare* was built and the gardens were laid out with tropical flowers, shrubs, and trees from the ends of the Earth, Ferdinand Maximilian became Maximilian I, Emperor of Mexico. He was transplanted, so to speak, by a coterie of Central American royalists, following the invasion of the country by France, Spain, and Britain, who were keen to get Mexico to pay its debts. It all ended rather badly in 1867 when poor Maximilian was executed by a republican firing squad at Cerro de las Campanas, near Santiago de Querétaro.

The transplantation of an Austrian arch-duke to Mexico was unsuccessful, but his tropical plants flourished on the Adriatic, just as plants and trees gathered from all over the world grace most English gardens. Arum lilies from Lesotho and Swaziland, trilliums from Appalachia, ginger lily from India, chusan palm from Japan, along with bamboo from Hunan in China. All of them rejoicing in tongue-twisting Latin names in the system of botanical classification pioneered by the Swede Carl Linnaeus in the middle of the eighteenth century, when merchants were bringing back exotic flowers, shrubs, and trees from all over the place. Linnaeus published his book, *Systema Naturae,* in Leyden, Southern Holland, in 1735, organizing plants (*regnum vegetabile*), animals (*regnum animale*), and minerals (*regnum lapideum) into* a comprehensive system, which grew larger and larger as specimens of strange plants, animals, and rocks, gathered by sailors, botanists, and merchants, poured into Europe throughout the eighteenth century.

A couple of centuries earlier the Swiss botanist Johann Bauhin collected and listed many plants known to him, and by the seventeenth century, this knowledge began to expand exponentially, but his book, *Historia plantarum universalis,* put together mainly in the sixteenth century, was not published till 1651, almost 40 years after his death.[5] All this vast effort of isolated scholars, united by the collecting efforts of merchants and sailors, culminated in the eighteenth century in what became known as "cabinets of natural curiosities" – the forerunners of public collections in museums – kept by merchants and gentlemen in their homes and workshops, in which specimens of plants, animals, shells, and minerals from the world over were gathered together, and sometimes cataloged in lavish collections of drawings and paintings illustrating the things collected and owned.[6]

So the distinctive thing about the history of our culture – the culture of commercial or capitalist society – is its geography; the total way in which it encompasses and embraces the entire globe. We now even have pictures from beyond the Earth, and no doubt sometime fairly soon, photographs from the outer planets, to join those images we've already created from the farthest reaches of the Solar System.

It's the plenitude, the seemingly infinite variety, the density of our cultural reference that is so bewildering, and gets us into so much trouble. Recently, a white lad with his blonde hair in rather fetching dreadlocks was berated by "identiterian" enthusiasts, for "cultural appropriation."[7] The young man's offense was apparently his cheek and arrogance in copying the hairstyles of Afro-Caribbean or Africans. He was simply appropriating the style of black people for his own "trivial" purposes of style or fashion. The mind boggles at this nonsense. Are we to go around berating Japanese and Nigerian men for wearing business suits pioneered in Europe and North America? I don't think so. Everything from Jazz to Hip-Hop, and Opera to Rap would be inconceivable without the mixing and intermixing of experiences from different places, both psychological and geographical. There'd be no Fela Kuti, no Afrobeat without cultural appropriation. Those "pesky" Japanese have even appropriated "the essentially American project of the comic book" with their manga, or *whimsical pictures*. Or did they? Something like manga were going the rounds in Japan from the twelfth or thirteenth centuries, coming to the fore again during the nineteenth. It's a moot point "who is appropriating who."

The reason for this is that the reality of cultural borrowings across the world does not result simply in a *mashup* of discrete elements, but in the very process of cultural mixing, entirely novel and unanticipated forms are developed. This is true in music, architecture, literature, fine art, popular cinema, comic books, philosophy, religion, and computer gaming. Not only geographically from one place to another, but also from one form to another. Computer games have grown from Pong in 1972, to the full in-depth, multi-dimensional interactive games of today. There has been vexed discussion over the years, among those who know about such things, about whether computer games are simply "the next step" from film and television, or an entirely novel form of art. Some years ago, Henry Jenkins even suggested that games and gaming are in a "transmedial state" – between all the older forms of narrative presentation.[8]

Whatever the case was 20 years ago, it is clear that player participation, not simply in the "gaming" aspect of games, but taking part in the direct development of the narrative is certainly a novel departure.[9] Many games are now "open world," and the stories and narratives are entirely player driven on a collaborative level, involving thousands, if not millions, of players. Star Citizen, Stellaris, No Man's Sky, and Elite Dangerous are good examples of this.[10] There can be little doubt that an entirely new form of art is developing.

New forms are produced and reproduced with a fecundity unequaled in history. It's no wonder that we are dazzled and often confused, because tracing the roots and origins of particular cultural forms is extremely challenging, to say the least. Consequently, the "identity warriors," worrying about "cultural appropriation," as they attempt to nail everybody's feet to the floor, have their work cut out in a political endeavor that is not only stupid, but is absurd because of its radical impossibility. The culture of commercial society is simply unimaginable without its worldwide appropriations.

This is as much true of our sciences and technologies as of our arts and entertainments. Technologies as different as paper making, printing, or ships that combined a keel with a sternpost rudder would not have been possible without diverse cultural influences – borrowings from around the world, that made entirely new technical departures possible. Without "al" this, and "al" that, from medieval Arab scholars and mathematicians, there'd be no *algebra* or *algorithms*. Without Charles Babbage and Ada Lovelace, no Alan Turing, and without the Egyptian Mohamed M. Atalla and the Korean Dawon Kahng, working at Bell Labs in the 1950s and early sixties, no modern electronics, integrated circuits, or Silicon Valley. Without Tim Berners-Lee at CERN in Switzerland, no world-wide-web. Without IBM no Microsoft, without Apple no personal computers, smart phones, and much else. The history of these electronic and digital technologies, concentrated largely in the United States, is produced from truly global influences, and expert scientists and engineers from all over. Materials, mines, and manufacturing plants are now strung across the world in integrated networks.

Complex supply-chains – the distribution of component manufacturing at a number of different sites in different countries and on different continents – have become economic because of transport innovations over the last 50 years. The most important of these has been the containerization of shipping and cargo handling, which started in the mid-fifties. On April 26, 1956, a crane lifted 58 aluminum truck bodies aboard an aging tanker ship moored in Newark, New Jersey. Five days later, the *Ideal-X* sailed into Houston, where 58 trucks waited to take on the metal boxes and haul them to their destinations.[11]

Although containers of different sizes and designs had been in existence since the 1930s, and possibly earlier, this shipment of cargo on the *Ideal-X* signaled the beginning of the end of dock labor as it had been known since the 1880s, and in many of its features, for centuries before that. Gradually, transport companies and manufacturers opted for the use of containers over the shipping of loose cargoes, in sacks, nets, and boxes. Containers could be packed at factories or warehouses – well away from the docks, dockers, and their stormy trade unions, well away from Byzantine payment schedules, and interminable disputes concerning the precise nature of mixed cargoes, and specific freight and handling charges. Despite bitter strikes and disputes, dockers from Liverpool to London, and longshoremen from New York, to Hong Kong and Sydney, on to Valparaiso, were roundly defeated as shipping companies introduced the new system, designing and building new cranes and derricks, and new port facilities, with better rail and road connections, to handle purpose-built container ships, which have, since the advent of computerized logistics, grown in size and sophistication.

Fairly soon container ships will be stripped of their residual crews as they sail the world's oceans, guided by onboard computers and sonar-assisted global positioning. No doubt the cost of transporting components from one manufacturing site to another, or from assembly to wholesalers, and thence to the final customers, will fall even further. It is the astronomical savings made since the 1970s by the speed of unloading, loading, and the turnaround of container ships that together with the disappearance of dockers, and reduction of crew sizes, has made modern global supply-chains both practicable and economic.

The other effect has been the freeing up of prime land for development along the rivers and waterways of all the world's large towns and cities. Everywhere from New York to Manchester former docklands have been transformed by the building of upscale waterside apartments. New urban spaces with public buildings, offices, entertainment, and cultural facilities have replaced the warehouses and cranes along old trading waterfronts throughout the world. Such additions to many cities have had the effect of strengthening a new urban culture, transforming the status and desirability of open-plan modern apartments, floor-to-ceiling windows, and the drama of high-rise living, in buildings often equipped with gyms, swimming pools, and roof terraces.

The new lifestyles of the urban middle class are, as a matter of course, largely restricted to the young and the well-to-do. However, the mass consumption of goods and aspirational lifestyles are spread far and wide, whether in the form of soft furnishings, the possession of electronic devices, or simply in activities like DIY – we browse those enormous emporiums stocking many thousands of items from screws, unfathomable gizmos, to lightbulbs, pot plants, and garden furniture. These myriad objects are carefully designed, manufactured, and transported across the world to our local B & Q, Menards, or Home Depot, at bargain prices.

We recreate, as best we can, the signature of the life we wish to lead, the kind of person we would like to be. Whether that's a scruffy intellectual wearing a wooly knitted hat who loves Reggae and rush matting, or a svelte mover and shaker with a minimalist penchant for a lack of clutter, there is something for everyone. We can be whoever we'd like to be. This is, at least, the offer, and we play it out in restaurants – fast food joints, popular eateries, fine dining – in pubs, bars, and coffee shops. On the street, we can in our mind's eye see ourselves performing in the ads as we live out our daily lives in spectacular fashion, presenting ourselves to the world, running in charity events, tumbling with our happy, healthy kids in the garden, striding out in panama hat or baseball cap, carrying a Louis Vuitton bag, or a knock-off Chanel.

There is no escape from the artifice. Everyone has become somewhat "camp" whether or not they realize it. Burly working-class men can now be seen in shopping streets carrying fashionably slim carrier bags with purchases from very expensive stores. In the past this would have been unthinkable. I remember in the 1960s working in shoe shops in South Yorkshire at a time when miners' wives would have to take a pair of men's shoes out onto the pavement for their waiting husbands to decide whether or not they liked them – the husbands would simply not enter the shop to inspect the shoes for themselves. No doubt they were embarrassed to enter such an unfamiliar and intrinsically feminine environment. In complete contrast, today there is a posture, a lifestyle, for everyone, even the beggars and their dogs in doorways have a singular way of presenting themselves to all and sundry.

This state of affairs is, no doubt, aided by the saturation of society by photographs and advertising. Not even Stalin or Hitler could have dreamed up the enormous images of beautiful men, glamorous women, and really desirable laptops that adorn billboards the size of houses, or in larger form, cover the entire sides of big buildings. Moving images are mounted high above the street on gantries, or in small electronic panels lining escalators and walkways. We swim round and around like goldfish in a bowl, in and out of magic castles, past phony rocks and plastic mermaids. Yet, it is all entirely real. Or is it? The life of the truly glamourous, of the super-rich, remains the stuff of fantasy, ubiquitous, ever-present, unrealizable, and yet we know that the promise is both as real and as ungraspable as the potential on offer.

It's usual on the left, and among socialists in general, to regard advertising as false, trivial, and unnecessary. This outlook is produced by a failure to grasp the infinite nature of desire on one hand, and fully understand the nature of capitalist production on the other. Two or three hundred years ago, the owners of cargoes arriving in London or New York might place a notice in a gazette or weekly newspaper announcing that they had a quantity of calico or tobacco or wine for sale at a named wharf or quay, or at a particular warehouse. The notice would be aimed squarely at merchants, shop keepers, and other wholesale buyers. Before the gradual rise of mass consumption, advertising aimed at the final consumer did not exist – the encouragement to buy was always aimed at middlemen, shopkeepers, or peddlers of one kind or another. Manufacturers and producers did not have to have a direct relationship with the public, their customers were suppliers to shops, not the end-users, or final consumers.

In France and the United States, advertising brokers or agents began to appear in a small way during the 1830s and 1840s, buying and selling space in newspapers, to shops and promoters of various products and services. But it was not until gradually rising living standards among working people during the last quarter of the nineteenth century that mass marketing of patent medicines, soap, sauces and relishes, tea, coffee, and cocoa began on a large scale. The makers and suppliers of these commodities had, for the first time, to establish brand and trade mark recognition among the general public. Confronted by the growth of mass market competition, manufacturers had, in order to realize profits from the sale of their goods, to establish a direct relationship with the final consumer. They had to create brand recognition for their products, and win repeated business and loyalty from their customers. This resulted during the 1870s and 1880s in the emergence of advertising in a recognizably modern form.

Since then, with mounting sophistication, year-on-year, decade after decade, advertising, brand promotion, sponsorship, and celebrity endorsement have become ubiquitous. From the days when later editions of the 1919 novel by Edith Maude Hull, *The Sheik*, carried a full-page photograph of the stunningly beautiful Rudolf Valentino as "The Sheik" in the Paramount picture of 1921, cross-over advertising, linking up different forms of product presentation has become routine. Perfumes, shoes, watches, clothing of all sorts, carry brand names and associations, glamour and quality stitched together, conspiring to stimulate desire, and the sense that we really can – all of us – participate to some degree in the luxury of commercial society.

It has always been par-for-the-course for socialist intellectuals, writers, and activists, for a hundred years or more, to tell working-class people not to be fooled by the blandishments of capital. "It's all false!" "It's all a fantasy, an illusion!" as if the mass of people are likely to welcome this miserable news. The truth is, of course, that most working people are fully attuned to the exaggeration, the irony, humor, and fun deployed by advertisers. Most of us have a fairly good eye and ear for the unmissable offers made, the interest free credit, and the real value of what it is we're buying. From a tea-towel bought from a street market stall, to one from a supermarket, or the household linens department of a big store, we know roughly how to estimate quality against price. By now most of us are experts at consumption and we know just how real the cornucopia of goods laid out before us actually is. What we are told about products is largely true. We know, too, that we're unlikely to be as good-looking as the lad in the ad in that shirt, but we'll look good enough. The fantasy on offer is worth aspiring to; it's a lot more appealing that the bloody socialist reality being offered by lefties who always want us to think about how awful everything is – we're well aware of that reality too – but what the capitalists offer is not only more fun in the here and now, it has considerably more sex appeal.

There is a very real problem with all of this, however. And that is debt. Debt and paying interest on loans are absolutely essential to the existence of commercial society. Capitalism could not exist without debt and interest payments. In previous kinds of society, like the Christian middle ages in Europe, charging interest was a sin, or was at least regarded as theft. Loans were widely made and interest was often, if secretly, charged. But it was not until the advent of commercial society that lending and the charging of interest was publicly practiced.

All investment is a species of loan; money is invested in a project in the seventeenth century, for example, to equip a sailing ship to sail from Delft to Macao to buy porcelain. The ship returns safely laden with rare and valuable Chinese crockery, and the investor gets back both the principal sum he advanced for the venture, and part of the profit realized from the sale of the bowls, jugs, and vases. Loans operate in a similar fashion, they are advanced by the lender in anticipation of future production – this future production is the means by which the borrower promises or guarantees repayment to the lender, plus the interest agreed when the bargain was struck. If the ship sinks or the borrower can't repay the loan, or even the interest on the loan – often called "servicing the debt" – then all hell breaks loose. Lawyers are consulted and contracts closely read. Debtors run and hide, and nowadays declare bankruptcy,[12] or make the best arrangements they can for restitution of the sum borrowed to the lender. It's a mess, but capitalism could not exist without lending, borrowing, and the payment of interest.

For almost the first 3 centuries of commercial society, none of this mattered to peasants, laborers, or workers. By and large, lending, borrowing, and interest payments were worried about by the bourgeoisie, by merchants, manufacturers, shipping companies, insurers, and banks. Indebtedness, where it existed among the population at large, was an informal private matter, between relatives, neighbors, and the keepers of small shops or taverns. People did not have lines of credit, or bank accounts of any kind.

This situation began to change during the nineteenth century, but most notably following the Second World War. It was then that the Tallyman, hire purchase, mail order catalogs, and the Provident Cheque[13] became the more common forms of credit that were made available to working-class people without bank accounts. Another, much older, or even ancient form of loan arrangement was provided by the pawn broker's shop. A valuable item is handed over as collateral in return for an agreed sum in cash – the item can then be redeemed with the payment of the sum borrowed, plus an agreed premium (or interest). I can remember a couple of visits to "Uncles" during my childhood. I was always fascinated by the three large golden balls hung up outside the store as the traditional sign for the business. My mum and dad, having spent-up everything taking us all to the seaside for a week, would return to London completely broke. So we'd get on the bus at Victoria Station and get off on the Kilburn High Road and go to a pawnbroker, "Uncles," where my parents would pawn their watches and rings, in order to get us all through from Saturday until Dad was paid in cash at the factory on the following Thursday.

This was not regarded as particularly dreadful at the time, because my mum would regale us with stories of the 1930s when people would pawn suits, shoes, and even blankets, in order to be able to buy groceries for their kids. In complete contrast, our post-holiday visits to the pawnbrokers were for the luxury of a week's holiday by the sea, not anything as desperate as mere survival.

However, everything has changed radically in the last 65 years. Now most workers have bank accounts, are paid monthly directly into their bank, and have access to credit in a great variety of ways, from new forms of the pawn shop – "cash generators" – current account overdrafts, store cards, credit purchases online, through to Mastercard and Visa. Credit has moved from being an essential element in running a business, handling investment shortfalls, and managing irregular cashflow, to a service routinely offered to the retail customers of banks, stores, and travel companies.

Lending and borrowing that in the past was largely "wholesale," so to speak, has today been extended to "retail." Ordinary customers, ordinary working people, are (excluding mortgages, car loans, or car leasing arrangements) routinely in debt. Many are carrying debt-loads it is extremely difficult for them to service, or to ever pay-off entirely. This has caused interminable anxiety for most folk regarding their outstanding loans. Mortgages and debts of all kinds also have the added bonus from the point of view of employers in making workers more compliant and fearful of being unable to meet their commitments if their income is threatened by industrial action or unemployment. Large amounts of debt have also had the paradoxical effect of helping to mask the stagnation of real wages, and of even raising the material standards of most working people's homes and lives throughout commercial society. This indebtedness is now intrinsic to our way of life, the "masses" have become fully integrated, in every sense, into the capitalist system.

Chapter 6

Fully Engaged

For most people, commercial society, or capitalism, if you prefer, does not involve "participation." By and large we don't think about the way we live as "taking part"; we don't think about our lives in abstract terms. We simply live in the here and now, worrying about the future, regretting the past, enjoying memories, hoping for the best. In these reflections, commerce is central to the cultural matrix within which the assumptions that frame our lives take shape. We don't often think much about this stuff. This is because, in general, we don't relate to the world as Marxists or revolutionary socialists; we don't think about "modes of production," but of ways of life. Commercial society is where we are, where we have always been. Capitalism is not a "mode of production" or some weird conspiracy of bosses against the workers, it's the fully functioning society in which we live. Most of us are well aware of inequality and injustice, but for most men and women these features are simply the inevitable consequences of people living together – they can get worse, or better, depending on the weather, earthquakes, tornadoes, tsunamis, pandemics, or the policies of governments, but they can't be abolished altogether.

The truth is, however, somewhat different from these working assumptions. History is fantastically popular in stories of the battling Plantagenets of fifteenth century England, to the kings and queens of the sixteenth, and on to the world wars of the twentieth. People are fascinated by the lives of cowboys and cattle barons, midwives in Limehouse and Bow in London's East End during the late 1950s, and just love misery fiction like Frank McCourt's *Angela's Ashes.* Tracing one's ancestry has also become a popular pastime, along with sending off for DNA tests to discover your genetic inheritance, finding out if you're more Viking than Celt, or just a rather dull mish-mash of Anglo-Saxon. Whether a person's ancestors hale from Africa, Asia, the Caribbean, or mainland Europe, the quest and interest in one's origins, of our historic families, is similar.

Strangely, all this historiographical industry and effort has little impact on how commercial society is popularly seen. It is as if commerce and capitalism have no history, it's as if the way we live now, *just is*. Of course, we know about the railways, about the industrial revolution, about dark satanic mills, of children up chimneys, and down coal mines with mum and dad, working in the flickering light of a candle, but commerce, the history of a society based more or less entirely on trade and trading, is rarely if ever approached by the general public.

It does, of course, have a history. Commerce has not always dominated production or ruled society in the way in which it began to do in the later years of the seventeenth century in the Netherlands and England. As it came into existence, free thinking and inquiry was greatly strengthened. Religious restrictions and exclusions became less rigid, and the right to criticize and discuss the doings of those in charge of government, and other public institutions, became decidedly freer for men of property.[1] And yet, from its earliest days, commercial society in the countries in which it first made its appearance were oligarchies. In England powerful groups of men, landowners, and merchants, related to each other by blood, or gathered together in associations, clubs, churches, parliaments, and the dining rooms of justices of the peace, joined the aristocracy in ruling the roost.

The result was a kind of hybrid system of rule in which intrinsically commercial relationships were masked by obligations, traditions, and habits, more akin to the aristocratic or feudal societies of the past. Consequently, the etiquette and social arrangements of eighteenth-century England present a peculiar mixture of subservience to past forms, together with novelty and innovation, in a society that enabled people to rise through the acquisition of wealth from trade or innovation, rather than blood or "breeding." By the early years of the nineteenth century, witty observers of this society, like the novelist Jane Austen, noted with irony the manner in which the obsession with money and breeding produced a corresponding need for those engaged in trade to learn the proprieties and manners of gentlefolk. However, nobody from outside of these closely connected elites had a say in how society was run.

The participation of laboring people, ordinary seamen, private soldiers, farm workers, miners, bricklayers, blacksmiths, stockmen, and cattle drovers was not required. The common people were excluded from active involvement in the public affairs of society. There was nothing new about this, previous kinds of society had always determinedly excluded the common folk from power and public decision-making. What was novel about commercial society was that from its inception, merchants, and manufacturers began to participate actively in the management of public affairs and the business of government. Politics, which had largely been the preserve of aristocrats and leading churchmen, now included, in a deeper sense, a much larger or wider group of men who were to be thought of as active citizens.

From 1716 regular general elections were instituted across England, Scotland, Wales, and Ireland. A great variety of local circumstances arose regarding elections for the following 116 years – until the first great reform act of 1832. Men without property were not always excluded – they might have the vote in a particular constituency, but certainly not in most. A great deal of money was often spent to ensure that the local grandees or bigwigs always won the election. Members of the oligarchy always remained in charge of elections, although the outlook and opinion of the local population was not inconsequential in determining which member of the elite won the seat. In the early part of the eighteenth century, great efforts were made by the grandees and big landowners to cement their privilege, by limiting access to parliament, against the sustained opposition of smaller independent landowners. E. P. Thompson in his brilliant article, 'Eighteenth-century English Society: class struggle without class?' explained the tension in the following manner:

> That constitutional defences against this oligarchy survived these decades at all is due largely to the suborn resistance of the largely Tory, and sometimes Jacobite, independent country gentry, supported again and again by the vociferous and turbulent crowd.[2]

This is a reference to the fact that elections could be rumbustious affairs, involving popular engagement at hustings, whether or not those enjoying the uproar had a vote or not.[3]

So by the 1720s, citizens, those men deemed to be full members of the "body politic," had grown in number, but still only accounted for a tiny percentage of the male population – perhaps no more than 4 or 5 percent in eighteenth-century England, Scotland, and Wales.[4] Despite riots, dissension, and repression, this continued to be the case, decade after decade until the reform of 1832. It was then that industrialization and the growth of very large cities began to exert their influence on affairs. By the middle of the 1830s it was realized that the leading citizens of emerging cities like Manchester, Birmingham, and Sheffield would have to find a place, not simply at the heart of the state, in the Palace of Westminster, but also in the management of their own town and city councils. Social stability required nothing less.

Yet the great majority of men and women, and particularly of working men,[5] continued to be thought of as having no stake in society, and therefore did not deserve a vote, or the right to stand for election to a city council, or to be represented in the London Parliament. Most men could not be trusted with citizenship because they had no real or substantial property. Their participation in the public affairs of the state or the community was not thought practical or welcome, by the grandees in the House of Lords, or by most of their allies in the Commons, and the city councils throughout the land.

This continued to be the case until the 1860s when it was becoming clear to many people in government and among the intelligentsia – novelists, public health officials, social reformers of all kinds – that something would have to be done to incorporate or introduce the bulk of adult working men into citizenship. There had been sustained struggles about extending the vote to lower-class men for 70 or 80 years, but by the mid-1860s matters were coming to a head. Serious disorder was feared if nothing was done.[6] The "brutish masses" teeming in fetid slums in Britain's large towns and cities were the stuff of nightmares for the bourgeoise, for the smart folks living in more favored neighborhoods. Then there were the mobs of mill hands, quarrymen, miners, laborers of all sorts, given to striking and rioting, combining against their masters in meeting rooms above pubs, planning God knows what. Then, the Irish, unimaginably squalid, perpetually violent. Fenians, one and all! [7] Irish laborers hovered forever in the mind's-eye of the English bourgeoisie during the nineteenth century as exemplars of barbarity and bestiality, "savages" a whole lot nearer than the heart of darkness. The least said about them, the better! Throughout Britain, from the West of Ireland to Glasgow, Bristol, Liverpool, Edinburgh, Manchester, and London, riot and revolt simmered very close to the surface. The exclusion of the majority of working men from political life was simply unsustainable if the commercial classes, the merchants, traders, "city fathers," the men of property were to sleep peacefully in their beds.

So it was that in 1867 the second great reform Act was passed. Adult men, tenants or lodgers, who paid at least £10 a year in rent were given the vote. In the countryside the owners and renters of very small plots of land also gained the vote and became citizens. This measure, in one-fell-swoop, doubled the size of the electorate in Britain from 1 million to 2 million, overnight. Attempts to prevent the new law from passing had led to the fall of the government, and were greeted by vast demonstrations organized by the International Workingmen's Association, the Universal League for the Material Elevation of the Industrious Classes, and the Reform League. In spring 1866, there was even wild talk of civil war, and a huge turbulent crowd fought the police to a standstill and occupied Hyde Park for 3 days. Troops were called, but kept in reserve, and despite the death of a policeman, further widespread bloodshed was averted.

Reform and good sense prevailed as the rulers of commercial society realized they could no longer remain securely in charge without the participation of working-class men in public affairs. The act of 1867 finally conferred citizenship on a very large swathe of working men, and the propertied classes secured the social stability that they desperately needed. The great reform was followed by the Forster Education Act of 1870, which initiated free elementary education for working-class children between the ages of 5 and 13, and a year later trade unions, whose members had hitherto had to duck and weave for decades, suffering repression by the employers, militias, and the police, were finally legalized.

The strategy of incorporation became well established, eventually widening the electorate through a series of reforms, until all working-class men got the vote irrespective of rent payments or property qualifications by 1918, and all women by 1928. Slowly but surely, it was realized that industrial society could only be securely governed if the consent of the mass of working people was actively sought, and this could only be gained if the working class was granted the right to participate in society as citizens, with at the very least, formal equality before the law with the rich and powerful. Oligarchies of the well-to-do and the well-connected continued to run the country, and continue to do so to this day, but they can no longer rule without the active consent of the working class.

This is the historical peculiarity of commercial society; everywhere that capitalism became well established the rule of law began to prevail. The sanctity of contracts and protection of citizens from the arbitrary acts of the wealthy and state officials became enshrined in political doctrine and legal practice. These commitments exposed brutal contradictions within the system. Hand-in-hand with the growth of commerce, and freer public discourse, came the trade in African slaves destined for the Caribbean and the Americas.

Slavery, of course, is an ancient institution which was practiced universally for millennia. However, with the birth of capitalism the practice of slavery became peculiarly vicious and intense, driven as it was by the desire to realize commercial profits primarily from the production of sugar and cotton on large plantations specifically organized around the super-exploitation of enslaved Africans. For more than 300 years the need for servile labor in the Caribbean, Brazil, and the southern United States resulted in the buying and selling of black men, women, and children on an "industrial" scale.[8]

Yet by the 1780s in England, this commerce in human beings began decisively to collide with an emerging fear of the "Divine Judgement of the Lord" falling adversely upon the British people and empire.[9] This fear undergirded the impulse or moral sensibility toward democracy; it produced not only the idea of extending the vote to white working men regardless of income or property, but the onset of the struggle for the abolition of the enslavement of black people. As a result, the trade in slaves within the British Empire was banned in 1807, and chattel slavery itself was declared illegal in 1833. These developments were integral to the growth of the democratic idea and the struggle to realize truly lawful forms of government. As early as 1829, "Policing by consent"[10] went hand-in-hand with aspirations for government by consent, as it slowly dawned on the capitalist class that in the long run, private property and stability could only be safely secured by the involvement of the mass of working people in the public affairs of society.

Such developments not only included the abolition of the trade in slaves, and of slavery, but also the great reform acts of 1832, 1867, and 1884. There were numerous attempts at the improvement and regulation of working conditions too, from *The Health and Morals of Apprentices Act* of 1802, through to those of the 1830s concerning working hours, the welfare of child laborers, and conditions in cotton mills, which together with numerous public health measures supported a growing recognition that it was a key responsibility of the state to extend its protection to the population at large, not simply to the influential and well-heeled. In any event it was becoming apparent by the 1820s and 30s that the protection of the well-to-do from infectious disease could not be secured without improving the social welfare and sanitary conditions of the poor. The national cholera epidemic in Britain, which began in October 1831, revealed the extent of the danger inherent in ignoring the living conditions of the laboring people in a rapidly urbanizing country.[11]

Dictatorships and *coup d'état*, together with disregard for the living conditions of the poor, have capsized many a capitalist country over the years, but democracy – government by consent – has been found to be the most effective way to guarantee social stability in densely populated societies founded on the ownership of private property, and relentless buying and selling. Citizenship, consent, and participation have preserved the social order, despite the life of commercial societies being racked with inequality and injustice.

This is where we find ourselves now in the twenty-first century; most working people are deeply committed to the defense of private property. This is rather more than a simple acceptance of the "way things are," but a heartfelt belief that we all have a fundamental right to own stuff. Most men and women do not make a distinction between "consumption goods" on the one hand and "capital" on the other. Although many millions do not own capital – property or money invested in businesses – they do own or rent their apartment or house, they value their cars, curtains, soft furnishings, "consumer durables," electrical goods, clothing, savings, books, and ornaments. They believe passionately that these things which they own and use should be protected by law and the police. They are not fans of looting or burglary, and they definitely do not believe in having fewer police on the streets or replacing cops with social workers or vigilantes. Some revolutionary socialists continue to flirt with the idea of popular policing carried out by a people's militia of some sort. This is imagined in the context of widespread rejection of state authority in favor of direct control by local committees. But this remains imaginary because it attracts no popular support whatsoever. The kind of communal organization needed to carry out such a scheme is not only entirely absent, it would be regarded at present by most people (if they'd heard of such a proposal) as simply absurd, impractical, and positively dangerous.

Because we are governed by consent, we obey legislation, and by and large support the courts and police in upholding the law. It is true that some communities are more suspicious or critical of the police than others, but on the whole, even in poverty-stricken communities and those suffering from the effects of racism or other kinds of discrimination, law enforcement by the police is generally preferred over the domination of the neighborhood by drug dealers or other criminals. School governors, police and community liaison committees, councilors, MPs, vicars, mosque leaders, rabbis, and many others participate in keeping lines of communication between the authorities and the general population as open and articulate as possible. The negative aspect of this approach – focusing on religious identity – often masks genuinely common concerns regardless of ethnicity. It is also true, of course, that many of these initiatives are subject to manipulation by religious leaders, together with local government and police agencies, resulting in cosmetic rather than real communication with the communities being policed.[12]

Despite these problems, there is a close relationship between the maintenance of law and order and participation in the ordinary life of commercial society. Attempts to improve housing and public health, along with free elementary education, were central to the project of incorporating the working class fully into the system. During the second half of the nineteenth century, investors in bricks and mortar were brought on board with the development of "five percent philanthropy"; the Peabody Trust (1864), Guinness (1890), and others built a large number of homes for rent.[13] Home ownership was also introduced into the mix. As early as 1872-3, Frederick Engels noted that a few better-off workers were able to take out rental-purchase mortgages on especially favorable terms offered by the Birkbeck Building Society of London's Chancery Lane.[14] Engels was pretty clear that initiatives of this sort could not ever remedy the housing shortage among working people. However, his skepticism did not dampen the enthusiasm of George Jacob Holyoake, who in 1879 sang the praises of the building societies being established for poorer people:

> The societies have taught a healthy frugality [its members] never else would have known; and enabled many an industrious son to take to his home his poor old father – who expected and dreaded to die in the workhouse – and set him

> down to smoke his pipe in the sunshine in the garden of which the land and the house belonged to his child.[15]

George was being optimistic to say the least, but his view of efforts to give the workers security by accumulating assets was evidently an important goal. In pursuit of this objective, the Co-operative Permanent Building Society was established to encourage home ownership in 1884 in order:

> ...to provide a further aid to co-operation and the public generally in the practice of thrift, the more comfortable housing of working people and the accumulation and profitable investment of capital.[16]

These early efforts, and the ideas that inspired them, have been relentlessly pursued to this day. It has nowadays resulted in the fact that almost two-thirds of the population either own their own house or apartment outright, or are buying homes with a mortgage. These millions are property owners and automatically seek the protection of the law, through the use of contracts, Her Majesty's Land Registry, wills, bequests, inheritance, and the employment of solicitors. This means that interest in the movement of house prices is both active and widespread – developments in the neighborhood that might adversely affect the value of one's property become matters of local concern. Protests might be organized, and the relevant authorities door-stepped with pickets, petitions, and crowded consultative meetings.

Those who cannot afford to buy do not reject the idea of home ownership, but often noisily protest the injustice inherent in their inability to buy. They rent their homes from housing associations, local authorities, or private landlords. The terms of their tenancies are tightly defined in the lease or tenancy agreement signed by the tenant and the landlord on commencement of the rental. Disputes between tenants and landlords, notwithstanding, these documents are governed by law, and enforced by the courts. No doubt there are laws relating to landlords and tenants, which people often struggle to change, but those engaged in such battles do so to strengthen the law in their preferred direction, not to weaken it, or undermine the jurisdiction of the courts. The inequality of those standing on either side of a contract, whether of employment or a tenancy, has not resulted in the rejection of contract law.

The almost "sacred" nature of contracts, enforceable by law, are valued from the bottom to the top of society. In cities like London and Manchester, the arrival of great cohorts of foreign investors keen to park their money in apartment blocks and other properties is now almost commonplace. This is because rich people in elective dictatorships, like Russia, or tyrannies like China, seek to salt away some of their wealth well beyond the reach of the arbitrary actions of their own governments. The security afforded by the rule of law in well-established commercial societies is attractive to those keen to protect their assets.

This desire for protection also applies to masses of people with modest means. Those interested in securing credit agreements and consumer protection, when a service or good does not live up to that promised by the supplier, assume that they have recourse to legally enforceable rights. Because of this it is widely acknowledged by shopkeepers and service providers that returns and refunds should be made as quickly as possible, with as little fuss as possible, in order to avoid damage to the reputation of their business, and to rule out legal entanglements and costly litigation. Of course, this doesn't always work, customers can be badly let-down or swindled, small businessmen can find it difficult to recover what is owed them, even when they have received the support of a court order. Things can always go wrong, and frequently do, but very few people indeed think that the failures of the system should lead us to dispense with law and order.

We should not minimize the grievous nature of the failure of the legal system to protect people from rank criminality, over-mighty companies, and impenetrable bureaucracies. One need only think of a black child dying in a squalid stairwell,[17] stabbed to death by gang members, or of a young lad slaughtered by racists at a bus stop[18] to gage the failure of the law to connect properly or articulately with the wider society it is supposed to serve. It was ever thus. Just *Google* "Aberfan," "Ronan Point," "Flint Michigan Water Crisis," "Abandoned Mines Drainage" in the US, "Thalidomide," the "Birmingham Six," and then remember the fire at London's Grenfell Tower; the examples of brutal injustice perpetrated within the rule of law are truly legion.

None of this catalog of misery, however, dislodges the engagement of most people with "the system." Working people not only increased their active participation in the life of commerce and commercial society by becoming citizens with the vote and formal equality before the law, but by becoming consumers. Now, of course, working people have always consumed and have throughout history even owned consumption goods, like their clothes, a few sticks of furniture, or a favorite book or family Bible. However, by the later decades of the nineteenth century and the early years of the twentieth, workers and their families experienced a gradual rise in real living standards as industry advanced, trade unions got stronger, and the *real price* of goods began to fall (regardless of rises in nominal prices). We can also tell from the emergence of widespread advertising of medicines and foodstuffs, the growth of music halls, of football clubs and associations, the ubiquity of Methodist and other non-conformist congregations – often supported with significant contributions from churchgoers in working-class neighborhoods – that disposable income was rising.

Even during the 1920s and "hungry thirties" in England, with the vast suburbs of bow-fronted houses, dolled-up with "Tudor" features and front doors boasting sunrise glass panels, poorer workers were buying newspapers, wireless sets, biscuits, and going to the pictures as least once a week. Following the defeat of the Labour Party government in 1951, post-war austerity policies were abandoned by the Tory government, and mass consumption really took off – this had occurred much earlier in the United States – but it became significant in Britain by the mid-1950s. Buying stuff and being blitzed by advertisers are key indications of engagement and participation in commerce and commercial relations. Despite grumbles about "keeping up with the Joneses," at no point have working people ever expressed popular disapproval of owning refrigerators, vacuum cleaners, gramophones, cameras, telephones, or of visiting the barber's, hairdressers' salons, teashops, or watching television. Indeed, the struggle of workers in trade unions during the fifties, sixties, and seventies was for higher wages and higher disposable incomes. People went on strike so they could afford better housing, better holidays, more and better consumption goods. The perennial struggle between capital and labor, employees and employers is invariably focused on the price to be paid for labor, a commercial question of abiding interest to the working people everywhere.

The commercial character of wage bargaining is spontaneously masked by the necessity, rhetoric, and iconography of solidarity. Without workers sticking together, wage bargaining cannot succeed. Perhaps inevitably moral purpose was invariably associated with the demands of strikers. As a consequence, many socialists, and the left more generally, have been entranced by the fortitude displayed by workers in struggle, dazzled by the potential of industrial disputes, and have placed positively barmy expectations of the social changes striking workers might be capable of bringing about. It is true, of course, that some labor disputes are fielded because of attempts by employers to speed up the pace or intensity of labor. Strikes have often been fielded in opposition to the introduction of new technologies or novel work practices.

The disappearance of typing pools, of typesetting and related print technologies, of traditional dock labor, of coal mining, and much else have often wracked the labor movement. But none of this undermines or weakens the commercial nature of the push and shove between workers and bosses over the terms on which one side sells her/his labor power to the other. Trade unions arose with commercial society during the earliest phase of industrialization, and what were initially called "combinations" proved to be an enduring and brilliant response by laboring people in both town and country to the severely commercial arrangements under which they were required to work for the rising bourgeoisie of manufacturers and coal owners, tenant farmers, gentleman landowners, and merchants of all kinds. Combinations of workers and "collective bargaining" are venerable institutions, which perpetually define and redefine the commercial terms upon which one side works for the other.

It is true that there are now new strains and novel circumstances associated with the break-up or retreat from industry and heavy engineering, which I will discuss more fully in the next chapter, but let's take it as read that working people are fully on board with commerce. Perhaps one of the most striking changes that has occurred is the arrival of large-scale retail banking. I remember well being paid in cash every Friday in a little brown envelope that was brought around on a tray of pay packets by someone from the office. In my first job I asked to be paid in ten-shilling notes – I was 15 and the idea of 14 banknotes was just heaven. Now, of course, all that has gone with the emergence of mass retail or personal banking. From the middle of the 1950s more middle-class people started using bank accounts and within 10 or 12 years this trend began to spread to more working-class people. The use of mainframe computers and database management systems facilitated the trend toward mass banking. In 1965 IBM developed a magnetic strip capable of storing readable information – within a year Barclay's introduced a hole-in-the-wall machine capable of issuing cash by use of a token, by 1968 the ATM had arrived. I can remember the experience of witnessing a friend using one in the early seventies.[19] Getting cash out of the wall at ten o'clock at night: simply astonishing!

Technical innovation and accompanying social changes led to more and more working people opening bank accounts, and their employers immediately took note of the savings that they could make by paying wages directly into bank accounts rather than paying for cash-handling and related security. By 1980 or thereabouts this transformation was well underway as more and more workers had accounts; wage packets were phased out in favor of bank transfers. It was a process that went hand-in-hand with the expansion of university and college attendance – where in the UK local authority grants had to be paid directly into bank accounts. This resulted in an entire cohort of young working-class people, often known as "non-traditional students," opening bank accounts almost as a right-of-passage on going off to university. Whatever they were as students, they were certainly non-traditional customers of banks and financial services.

This readiness of workers to buy into financial services has, apart from overdrafts and the use of credit and current account cards, resulted in the widespread use of savings instruments and pensions of various kinds. Yet almost 7 percent of the British population have no savings, while a further 18 percent have less than a thousand pounds saved. However, two-thirds have savings worth between 10 and 12 thousand pounds. This is unevenly distributed between different areas and regions of the country, with folk in London saving the most, and women everywhere typically saving 50 percent less than men.[20] Millions of people with extremely modest means also contribute to private pensions of one kind or another in the hope that they will be able to supplement the basic retirement pension paid by the state when the need arises.

According to Her Majesty's Revenue and Customs, average contributions to "personal pensions," now subject to automatic enrolment, are running at around £2700 per year. Almost 10.5 million contribute to personal pensions, that are unlikely to pay much on retirement and will prove inadequate unless the individual is able to afford further top-ups via private or company pensions, or through a buy-to-let property, or some other investment instrument. Despite these difficulties and the loss of company pensions, or the erosion of their final value, as a result of fraud or fast practice by employers, workers continue to attempt to make provision for the future as best they can, and show no sign of rejecting commercial society, for all its problems, inequality, and injustice.

Notwithstanding widespread difficulties and popular rage, over the last 150 years working people in Britain have been incorporated fully into the operation of commercial society, first as citizens and then as participants in all of the multifarious aspects of the life and culture of capitalism, governed or directed by buying and selling, the defense of private property, and respect for the rule of law. Even during the worst times, the embattled 1980s, great swathes of the working class were clearly on board with Margaret Thatcher and the powers that be. Coal continued to be mined by men who rejected the strike called by the National Union of Mineworkers, and Thatcher's introduction of the right of tenants to buy their council houses (project apartments and houses) was enormously popular. The fierce critics of commercial relations, the revolutionary socialists, anarchists, and the more moderate left, have been perpetually dismayed by this reality, as all their aspirations for the overthrow of capitalism have been sabotaged by the working class rather than the bourgeoisie.

Chapter 7

An Imaginary Working Class

Phrases like "The working class," or even worse, "the class," have a distinctly antique ring to them. They seem to conjure up a time when brawny men and robust women – *Rosie the Riveter* types – toiled away in shipyards, factories, and mines. I well remember, as a "mature" university student in the early 1970s, standing at one end of a bridge in Barrow-in-Furness, with my bundle of *Socialist Workers*, waiting for a veritable wave of workers to flow toward me across the bridge from the shipyard. The men, at the end of their shift, came in a dense crowd, the youngsters running in groups, half a dozen motorbikes, flocks of cyclists out in front, and a few cars slowed and crowded by those walking purposefully home. My papers did not "sell like hot cakes," but I used to shift quite a few, and successfully convened meetings with a number of workers to discuss Tony Cliff's book, *The Employers' Offensive: Productivity deals and how to fight them.*[1] Then, a year or two later, I came out as gay, and my career as a revolutionary became decidedly muddled. The leadership of the International Socialists[2] were distinctly unimpressed by my carry-on in an Afghan coat, large gold earrings, and shoulder bag – "acceptable man bags" were still some years off.

Despite the success of a few of my meetings convened to discuss sexuality with shop-stewards, our leaders took the view that I was letting the side down so I was arraigned before my branch officials. There were three of them, sitting behind a table in a comrade's kitchen. A chair was placed in front of the tribunal for me, and the discussion commenced. The upshot was that I was bringing the party into disrepute by supporting resolutions favoring wider political discussion, and by my political work on gay liberation. Activity around the rights of homosexuals was inconsistent with the organization's priorities. I was, therefore, ordered not to engage in any more work on gay liberation, but to confine myself instead to the branch's "textile fraction." This meant handing out leaflets and selling papers at factories and tailoring workshops in the West Riding of Yorkshire.

Unsurprisingly, we parted company soon after, but I still had time to publish my 19-page pamphlet *The Politics of Homosexuality*, which argued that gay liberation would be impossible without the collapse or overthrow of capitalism.[3] So although I'd been thrown overboard by IS, I remained committed to the inspiring idea of the seizure of power by the workers, which very rapidly collided with the much more libertarian ideas embraced by the "brothers and sisters" of gay liberation. Who, despite a generous commitment to the common emancipation of everybody in sight, had very little time or patience for traditional notions of the workers or the working class. As things have turned out, many of the militants of the gay liberation movement were well ahead of their time in anticipation of the emerging *zeitgeist*. However vague or confused their ideas sounded to me at the time, most gay liberationists knew that the game was up for what I would have called "class politics." They instinctively knew that profound changes were afoot.

They were to be proved right, and I was utterly confounded. The stormy working class of the seventies of the last century, the striking dockers, coal miners, car workers, and the women on strike for 2 years at Grunwick film processing laboratories at Dollis Hill in London were not the future, but almost the last hurrah of the industrial working class in Britain. The *dénouement* came in the following decade with the decisive defeat of the great miners' strike, followed by that of the print workers at Wapping. A combination of cheaper coal from opencast mining and the digitalizing of print technologies put paid to what Harold Macmillan had once described as "The Brigade of

Guards" of Britain's trade unions. He was referring, of course, to the National Union of Mineworkers, and by extension to the best organized, wealthiest workers in the most hidebound of trades: printers. They were well-organized, maintained a *closed shop*, and engaged in a truly Byzantine range of measures to enhance their earnings, and ensure that their sons got jobs.[4]

The typesetters on the daily newspapers had traditionally ducked and weaved in the face of their employers, who could rarely risk production delays to the output of daily newspapers on Fleet Street. By moving all of his national titles to a new plant in Wapping, free of "closed shop" agreements, Rupert Murdoch and News International put paid to hot metal typesetting as the unions' arcane procedures were swept away by new machines and methods. A total of 670 printers at Wapping replaced the 6800 workers that had been needed in the old-style printworks.[5] Both groups, the miners and the printers, were soundly thrashed by government and employers as Britain deindustrialized and began to use computers in more and more circumstances.

The industrial working class was robustly growing during the 1980s in China, South Korea, Japan, and at entirely new points of production scattered across the globe, while in Britain the working class appeared to be disappearing. This, of course, was an illusion. The working class was simply undergoing the profound changes demanded by commercial investors in the older industrial centers. Shipbuilding, heavy engineering, and mass component manufacturing were being transferred to more efficient, modern, and cheaper plants around the world, as the old centers of production in Britain were dismantled or left to rust. Henceforth, workers would be required to work in transport, logistics, administration, hi-tech manufacturing, and services in entirely new ways and in an entirely new atmosphere.

What happened in the eighties and nineties of the last century was the remodeling of the working class. This revealed the abiding truth that the working class is not the creation of its own consciousness, but of the needs of capital.[6]

Despite the heroic iconography and dodgy histories produced by revolutionary socialists and the left, the working class was never a fixed entity; it was always subject to the whims of the investing public, changes in technology, the fluidity of markets, and the resulting reorganization of businesses. The laboring people lovingly described and celebrated in 1963 by E. P. Thomson's *The Making of the English Working Class* were working at the dawn of the industrial age.[7] As steam locomotives and the railways arrived, circumstances changed rapidly. During the 1840s and 1850s, the working class described by Thompson disappeared to be replaced by people living, working, and organizing in radically different ways. This working class was renewed again during the last 20 years of the nineteenth century, as industry grew in scale and intensity. Women workers at the Bryant and May match factory at Bow, in London's east end, went on strike, demanding better conditions and the end of fines and penalties imposed by the company. The following year in 1889, the London docks came out on strike, demanding sixpence an hour. Developments of this sort meant that hundreds of thousands of unskilled laborers, in gas works and a variety of other jobs, were drawn into mass industrial trade unions, quite different from those of the more skilled and enfranchised male workers.

Commercial interests put their money where they think they can make a profit and they will employ working people in the roles which they regard as both necessary and appropriate to the job in hand. Consequently, during the second half of the 1980s and the early 1990s, coal mining and coal miners were replaced in the UK by logistics companies, warehouse workers, and truck drivers. The development of digital technologies led to the disappearance not only of typesetters and traditional printworkers, and of telegrams and telex, of comptometer operators, but of filing clerks too.

The white collared drones employed to calculate the discounts available to clients worked through piles of invoices with the aid of Odhner mechanical machines, until they were eventually replaced by electronic calculators, and then by a single formula in one cell of an Excel Spreadsheet. Typing pools and secretaries disappeared, as most managers began to be required to handle their own correspondence and diaries on personal computers, without the assistance of legions of smart young women, who were formerly hired for these tasks. Changes of this sort occurred throughout the late 1980s, the 90s, and the early years of this century. In every branch of industry upheavals of this kind were experienced as an entirely new working class was brought into being by the needs of the commercial interests that motivate and shape the economic life of the country.

This working class continues to be resolutely *working class*. It is composed of millions of men and women engaged in routine manual or clerical labor in jobs and workplaces over which they have little or no control. They work for wages determined, as of old, by the combination of supply and demand for particular kinds of skills and aptitudes, and by the efforts of trade union organizations to persuade employers to improve conditions and pay higher wages. Within the private sector, though, annual appraisal meetings, in which performance and wage levels are reviewed by managers with workers individually, are more common, because of the disappearance of trade unions and the attenuation of collective bargaining in most settings.

The densely collective nature of work in shipyards, typing pools, or on the factory floor has largely been replaced by jobs of an entirely different character. Today's workers typically work in relatively small teams or groups, regardless of the actual size of the firm, in which they are required to monitor each other's performance, and engage with the objectives of the enterprise in a manner inimical to older ideas of "us" and "them," and of the perpetual struggle between workers and the bosses. There are also sweatshops which pay below the minimum wage, there are workers on zero hours contracts, and there continue to be workplaces which maintain old-style disciplines with entirely new technologies, like call-centers, logistic warehouses, and postal and delivery services. However, workers hired as part of the core labor force today are expected to work together in a rather more collegiate manner than in the past, to train, police, and supervise each other, and to pay attention to the quality of their product or service, without the close hands-on supervision of the past, but with a kind of internalized commitment to the success of the firm.

Supervision, nowadays, is rarely carried out by charge-hands, progress-chasers, foremen, supervisors, chief clerks, first sales, or buyers, but by performance indicators. Most people have become "cost-centers," and weekly and monthly returns, or sales figures, provide managers and employers with reams of data which cannot be argued with. You are either earning your keep or you are not. An objective measure is ruthlessly insisted upon, both by employers and fellow workmates or colleagues, who are often alert to lackadaisical team members who might impose upon them by not pulling their weight. So the old solidarities in the face of the foreman have ebbed away, and been replaced by self-motivation and a much more individualized culture. Consequently, trade union membership has over the last 30 years declined, and workplaces have become increasingly hostile to the operation of notions like "collective bargaining," and solidarity. It is not that working people have become selfish or gripped by an every-man-for-himself outlook, but rather that they have developed a lively sense that their real interests are best served by the success of the firm, rather than that of the trade union, or some imaginary idea of class struggle. Of course, the tension between workers and employers often persists under the surface, with employees refusing to "take work home," or worry about anything beyond their contractual or formal commitments.

Things are radically different in rail transport and the public sector in the UK where trade unions remain relatively strong. Paradoxically, this is in organizations where the profits of private investors, independent of significant state subsidy, have little or no relevance. Commerce is often thought of as destructive of the abiding values of community and social solidarity. It is here that more traditional notions of class relations persist. It is much easier in this context for trade unions to operate than in the private sector, and the workers are often inspired and motivated by aspirations for public service and utility, fueled by ideas antagonistic or inimical to the profit motive or commercial objectives of any kind. However, even here commerce has been insinuated into the public sector, not simply by attempts to impose ersatz "market" performance indicators, drawn from comparisons with the private sector, but also by the engagement of a multiplicity of private firms and consultancies, brought in to provide specific services thought to be cheaper and more economic than those which might be provided by directly employed – and unionized – workers.

Despite these difficulties, the public sector in Britain has proved to be the last redoubt of socialists and committed left-wingers. It is among NHS workers at all levels, school teachers, university staffs, town hall and college administrators that many socialists and revolutionaries are to be found, sheltering from the bracing winds of commerce, with better pay and conditions than those offered for similar roles (where they exist) by private companies.

Working-class people nowadays not only find themselves in different kinds of jobs than might have existed 30 or 40 years ago, they live in extremely varied circumstances from grim tower blocks and rather forbidding housing estates and projects, to positively leafy middle-class style suburbs. They live in cramped flats and apartments, row houses, terraced streets, and spacious semi-detached houses with generous-sized gardens. They are homeowners, tenants, room-mates, flat-sharers, lodgers, and sofa surfers. These different living conditions and their related lifestyles reflect vastly different levels of income, insecurity, skills, and education. There are also important differences between the outlook and assumptions of people who live in villages and small towns, and those of the great cities.

Workers are not unified by employment or places of residence, they do not necessarily share countries of origin, mother tongue, or religion. Mass movements of people around the world have over the last 50 or 60 years radically altered the racial and cultural composition of the working class in Britain and Western Europe. We have towns which are not simply majority white, but are places where a black or foreign-born person is rarely if ever seen, and boroughs in which the majority of the population come from Africa or the Caribbean. There are areas in which the minarets of mosques, the domes and fluttering flags of Hindu temples, and the Gurdwaras of Sikhs outpace the congregations of gothic-revival Anglican churches, which quietly molder away, forgotten, as the enthusiasm of Christian evangelicals from Nigeria or Jamaica put them in the shade. Then there are neighborhoods in which the streets, morning and evening, are busy with Hasidic men with *peyot*, and the tassels of tallith prayer shawls showing beneath waistcoats and jackets, hurrying to drop off or collect their kids from school. Evidently there are no typical workers or typical working-class neighborhoods.

The analysis of the 2011 UK census released by the Office for National Statistics in July 2014 revealed that almost 26 million people were living as part of a couple, married, cohabiting, or civil partnered. Of this number, one in ten, or 2.6 million people, were in inter-ethnic relationships. This number had increased by around 2 percent over the previous 10 years, and we can have no reason for supposing that this trend is not continuing.[8]

To be sure, not all these people will be engaged in routine labor, some will be middle class, and some will no doubt be from the bourgeoisie; however, it is safe to assume that most will be working class. This level of diversity is permanently changing the make-up of our population and of attitudes about race and ethnicity.[9]

Something similar might be said about homosexuality. The widespread public acceptance of gay relationships and even of same-sex marriage represent profound cultural change taking place throughout the working class, and the country in general. It is true that changes in the status of women have been considerable over the last 50 years. I well remember my mum's outrage in around 1958 or 1959, that despite having a full-time job, she was not allowed to sign a hire-purchase agreement for a new suite of furniture – Dad had to go in on a Saturday afternoon to complete the deal. Battles of this sort had been fought by women since the 1850s.[10] The reform of laws and public attitudes toward homosexuality, however, were quite different and much, much, faster.

The ball was set in train in 1952 by the Church Information Board, which produced "The Problem of Homosexuality: An Interim Report," for the Church of England Moral Welfare Council. This led to the establishment of the Wolfenden Committee in 1954, which reported 3 years later. The committee recommended the limited decriminalization of homosexuality, and this finally occurred some 10 years later in 1967. The view of the Church of England and of Wolfenden was that the law should not intervene in the private life of adults, which at the time meant those over 21 years of age. Despite numerous battles waged by gay men and lesbians, and sustained lobbying by the "great and the good," over the next 35 years full civil equality was not achieved in England, Wales, and Scotland until 2014 (and in 2020 in the North of Ireland). An equal age of sexual consent with heterosexuals had been achieved in most of the

United Kingdom by 2000, and subsequent legislation was largely uncontentious and had the effect of merely clearing the statute books of discriminatory features aimed at the repression of male homosexuals.

Despite this 60-odd-year struggle, a very long time in the life of those of us involved, when viewed as history, the legal emancipation of homosexuals was remarkably rapid. In a single lifetime we went from being criminals, hunted, harassed, openly despised, and spat upon, to being free, equal, and even celebrated members of society. I well remember my feelings, for the first time, seeing young policemen and lads from the Royal Air Force marching in their uniforms in the annual Pride Parade in Manchester. I could scarcely believe my eyes. The pavements were packed with working-class people, many in family groups who'd brought their kids along to witness the fun and razzmatazz. By the opening years of this century, this was an astonishing reversal of our fortunes, and of the attitude of the mass of working people. It goes without saying that prejudice and repression continue to exist, small towns and more parochial places are not as quite at ease with homosexuality as the center of big cities, but the brutality and prejudice has been driven to the margins by extraordinary changes in the outlook, and public behavior, of the mass of the working class.

Perhaps the most signal change has been the untroubled and wide acceptance of same-sex marriage. In Britain, apart from the North of Ireland, the legal change which permitted the marriage of homosexual couples occurred almost without incident. There was very little agitation for it, no demonstrations or uproar demanding the reform. One can only conclude that it was changes in the nature of marriage itself among heterosexual couples that opened up the possibility of gays and lesbians being admitted to the institution. As marriage between men and women became increasingly about companionship, and was the free choice of two individuals, without any necessary permission, participation, or regard, from relatives, the rationale for excluding homosexuals began to ebb away. Of course, couples usually welcome the support and help of their respective families, but they no longer seek permission, and the marriage itself is simply a public celebration and marking by the couple of their intension to love, care, and support each other through thick and thin, despite everything that life might throw at them. As such, marriage stripped of its historical and religious baggage could include homosexual couples, and appear to be reasonable to great swathes of the public.

It is difficult to account for such changes, particularly given the conceit of the liberal intelligentsia who think of themselves as uniquely tolerant and world-open, in contrast to the mass of working people. The milieu composed of university teachers, writers, broadcasters, doctors, and lawyers often appear to think that people at the bottom of the social heap are intrinsically bigoted and backward. Indeed it has been beliefs of this sort that have over the years slowed down reform because of the fear in posh intellectual circles of negative reactions to the reform of manners and morals among the population at large. When I was coming out as gay in the early seventies, for example, it was common for older gay men I met to warn against public displays of homosexuality with the distinctly Edwardian phrase, "We mustn't frighten the horses in the street."[11] The idea that acceptance of homosexuality might be private, considered, and restricted to "educated" circles was embedded in this sentiment.

The conception that the highly educated, and those well-placed in positions of authority, have a more balanced, rounded, and rational view of social divisions than those at the bottom of the heap is certainly robust, but survey data does not provide satisfactory evidence one way or another. It remains an impression. This impressionistic stance was mobilized by many of those who voted "remain" in the 2016 referendum on the UK's membership of the European Union, with the argument that by and large those who successfully voted to leave the EU had been misled, were ignorant, xenophobic, and racist "Little Englanders." This has exposed a statistical mess created by the difficulty of disentangling "objective" class position from "subjective" class identification, and is further compounded by researchers deploying slippery categories like "libertarian," "authoritarian," and "socially conservative."[12]

However, the real experience, and honest presentation, of the second half of the twentieth century leaves us with a radically different account. The social and cultural changes that occurred between 1950 and the Millennium, regarding race, sexuality, the position of women in society, and the rights of the disabled, have, taken together, been truly astounding. The general outlook, the general sensibility, the general commitment to fair and equal working people.

These changes are immensely complicated, and must indeed have involved a myriad of influences, bold and clear, subtle and illusive. However, the startling alteration in the lives of people at work and in their neighborhoods, in the way they live now – the difference between how people lived in, say, the fifties and sixties of the last century – and in the third decade of this one, has altered most people's ready cultural assumptions about the rights of individuals, and the way we regard and treat each other beyond all recognition. The working-class life of those of us who grew up in the fifties valued homogeneity, sticking together, not getting above yourself, not being too ambitious, valuing social solidarity and community above all else. Difference of any kind was suspect and to be discouraged. The employers too, and the structure and regulation of the workplace, were hostile to difference and variation of all kinds. Difference was regarded as dysfunctional by all concerned until new technologies and the reformation of the workplace began steadily to eat away at the circumstances in which serried ranks were needed to do the same thing, at the same time, in the same way, always under close supervision.

As this older working class fearfully fought its rear-guard actions against new ways of working in the 1970s, and met its Waterloo in Britain during the years 1984-1986, a new working class came into being with a strikingly different outlook on everything from sexuality to home ownership. This is often attributed by lazy commentators to the contradictory or paradoxical successes of Margaret Thatcher, John Major, and Tony Blair – whereas the truth is that these prime ministers were merely the handmaidens or stewards of international investors who needed to shift resources into new technologies, and new ways of working, which in turn transformed the lifestyle and neighborhoods of millions of working people.

People in this new working class very rarely opt to go on strike, and appear to have little or no collective political presence. Different sections may exert pressure or influence in referenda and elections in contradictory ways, some people in some regions opting for one course of action, while other groups of working people take an entirely different approach to what might be perceived as common problems. This is a reflection of the extraordinarily broad character of working-class experience. People engaged in routine manual or clerical work do not form a homogeneous block; they're neither heroes nor the "salt of the Earth."

There are pockets of ignorance, fecklessness and disorganization at one end of the working class, and high levels of skill, intellectual, and cultural sophistication at the other end. Between these extremes there is everything from people engaging in amateur theater groups, to respectable older folk in blazers bowling on well-kept greens. Gardening or home improvement are significant endeavors. There are avid viewers and listeners to Public Service Broadcasting, BBC Radio Four, and those who never switch over from Radio One or their local music station. Millions tirelessly work for charities, for their church, for their synagogue, or mosque, fun-running, staffing food banks, crewing lifeboats, singing in choirs, or spending precious hours rehearsing with the local brass band. There are those who enjoy black-tie functions, uproarious hen-nights, trips to concerts of classical music, Broadway and West End musicals, or spending their weekends playing guitar in rock bands, or excelling in gaming on computers – I have even met a working-class dressage champion, whose day job was nursing the mentally ill. There is no limit to the variety of the opinions, prejudices, activities, or ambitions of working-class people. They are not the undifferentiated "masses" waiting to be told what most already know about commercial society by revolutionary socialists.

The working class of many a Marxist's imagination simply does not exist. Working people are not gathered together by employers in workplaces with common experiences and aspirations. Indeed, they never have been. When industrial labor concentrated large groups of men and women in factories and in proletarian neighborhoods, it often appeared to socialists, and even to bourgeois social reformers, that the working class actually existed as a veritable block of humanity, ready-made and waiting for "improvement" by clerics and do-gooders of one kind or another, or by agitators committed to stirring up the discontented to riot and revolution. As it has repeatedly turned out throughout the last 3 centuries, working people have not proved to be putty in anybody's hands. They have not made themselves available either to moralists and improvers, or to revolutionaries, promising them a starring role waving red flags in a transformative social drama.

There have indeed been many revolutionary upheavals in the past, a reality I will discuss in the conclusion, but for now, let's say that the spectacle of the working class dreamed up by the Salvation Army at one time, and communists at another, has rarely been able to grasp the vivacious plenitude of the social and cultural potential of the millions of men and women who work for wages in routine jobs in factories, offices, workshops, cafes, pubs, stores, and warehouses. The diversity of talent and creativity of "the masses" means that it is not necessary or possible to amalgamate this great crowd into a homogeneous social force of the imagination, for any reason whatsoever.

Conclusion

The Future of Communism

The major problem that we have, those of us on the middle, near, or far left, is not the Tories, the bourgeoisie, or the capitalists, call them what you will, but the working class. Our problem is the radical mismatch or disconnect between us, and the millions of people who do not have investments in banks or businesses. Those who have to live on wages or pensions are not at all impressed by our virtue or foresightedness. The whites among them do not feel responsible for slavery, or that they are committed racists because they are white. The blacks do not view themselves through the prism of victimhood, destined to be at the bottom of the heap either. The South and East Asians are not detained by leftist narratives of oppression; they just work hard and ensure that their kids do their homework and pass their exams. Women struggle along with their menfolk, loving them, fighting them when necessary, but always striving to work things out between each other and the circumstances and impositions that the world places on them and their kids. Similarly, homosexuals, lesbians, and gay men make their way as best they can, making full use of the freedoms and opportunities that equality before the law provides, and dealing with bigotry and prejudice as and when it arises. All these different elements within the working class are well aware of the problems, both specific and general, that they confront in commercial society, they really do not need us, the socialists, revolutionary or otherwise, to itemize their difficulties, or to tell them how to think about the society in which we all live.

Let's take it as read that we all live in commercial society, within a capitalist mode of life, which shapes us and often frames what we can and cannot do, and determines what we can, and cannot think. In 2009, Mark Fisher embraced this reality by opening his book, *Capitalist Realism*, with Fredric Jameson's observation that, "It's easier to imagine the end of the world than the end of capitalism."[1] This is undoubtedly true. Just as true as it was easier for peasants, together with well-educated divines, in the fourteenth century to imagine the "end of days," than it was for them to imagine the end of princes and their men-at-arms. It was ever thus, imagining radically different futures has always proved difficult, and because utopias are always conjured up using the intellectual resources available in "the here and now," they always carry with them the indelible marks of their birth at the time and place in which they were first imagined.[2] This is as true for Yanis Varoufakis in his troubling *Another Now*[3] in 2020, as it was for William Morris in the sunny uplands of his *News from Nowhere*[4] a hundred-and-thirty-odd years ago. Communism has never had any difficulty imagining the future; its problem has always been firmly in the present.

This is a present in which the working class by and large support the nation, believe that it is worth defending against all comers. In Britain most working people do not mouth platitudes like "my country, right or wrong," or wave flags, unless it's to help conjure victory for our national football teams.[5] But they do believe that Britain is a good place, more peaceful and law-abiding than other "less happier lands." Who can doubt this? While the left often bangs on about the iniquities of our country and its history, most of the population are well aware that Winston Churchill, a supporter of Italian fascism in the 1920s, was a war-mongering Tory bastard, who was brave and positively heroic in his resolute opposition to Hitler and Mussolini in 1940. He spoke up for the nation, and for the great mass of her working people at the time, and for that, he can be forgiven much. This goes for the rest of the brutal contradictions and perfidiousness of our national story. There was always an upside – we can always pit the Oliver Cromwell of the Parliamentary forces against the Cromwell of the massacre at Drogheda or the seizure of Jamaica; the Clapham Sect and the British Navy against the slave traders; Sir Robert Peel and his police against the yeomanry and drink sodden local militias; the Chartists against the Duke of Wellington; Tom Mann and Ben Tillett against the shipowners, and so on, back and forth throughout our history.

It is often said that the modern working class is culturally conservative. That they love the family and the community ties that often bind neighborhoods together. This is undoubtedly true. It is also the case that working men and women over the last 30 or 40 years have had to deal with endless technical innovation and the change that it brings to both the workplace and the way we live. Consequently, most working people have taken all this change in their stride. It is a key part of my argument that the working class is not a stable or static social bloc, but an ever-changing dynamic social reality, constantly on the move within the maelstrom of change which is a perpetual feature of commercial relations.

That there is also sustained and robust opposition to changes in work practices and to the introduction of new technology where it makes tasks more onerous, or threatens job security, is not in doubt. Workers have always resisted the changes arbitrarily imposed upon them by employers, but it is surely misleading to characterize this resistance as "conservative." Because the apparent atavism of workers, fighting against the novel impositions of employers, must always be balanced by the preparedness of working people to embrace startling cultural innovations and new ways of living. The truth is that working people have come to accept new ways of working as readily as they've accepted inter-ethnic marriages and relationships. They have often dragged their feet, but they've always embraced change. They have come to accept homosexuals in every walk of life, including a general, if unengaged, acceptance of equal marriage. They accept football managers and players from all over as long as they are successful, and ensure the ball hits the back of the net. The "conservatism" of the working class is as dynamic and subject to perpetual change and innovation as the rest of our society.

The capacity of the mass of our people for political discretion is vital in the face of threats like Islamic terrorism, which could spill over into chauvinism and violence against run-of-the-mill Muslims, who like the rest of the working class are much more interested in the welfare of their children than the death-cults spawned by their co-religionists. The irony and balance of most working-class people, when faced with racial or religious strife, is demonstrated in a great variety of ways. I well remember Mary, my mother-in-law (of my second marriage); she was a woman who had started work in a cotton mill at the age of 14, and had never traveled anywhere much. Mary in some abstract sense had racist opinions, but this did not prevent her from taking a greetings card to her elderly Muslim neighbors at *Eid al-Fitr*, the end of Ramadan, with the splendid explanation, "Well, it's their Christmas, isn't it?" I well remember an Irish woman, an old-fashioned "fem" lesbian, sitting in our gay liberation meetings in the 1970s carefully noting events down in her Roman Catholic diary. I'll call her Hannah. She was "as racist as the day is long," and when on one occasion I expostulated, "But Hannah, how can you say that, all your kids are black!" she just laughed and said, "Oh, that's different."

Like Mary and Hannah, we live in the midst of contradictions, of messiness, that will simply never fit the political strictures beloved by the left, and often insisted upon by revolutionary socialists. Consequently, much humor and many jokes will fail the leftist test. This is because we do not believe that virtue is the greatest prize, any more than we believe that gender is fluid, that biological sex is irrelevant, or that most Muslims are bad, particularly when they're good at football, like Mo Salah:

If he's good enough for you, he's good enough for me.
If he scores another few, then I'll be a Muslim too.
If he's good enough for you, he's good enough for me.
Sitting in the mosque, that's where I wanna be!
Mo Salah-la-la-la, la-la-la-la-la-la.

This ironic forbearance was even extended to club owners when Fulham fans used to sing about Mohamed Al-Fayed, the one-time owner of the club, of Harrods department store, and the father of Princess Diana's lover, Dodi:

Al-Fayed Wooo-ooo—oh
Al-Fayed wooo-ooo-ooh
He wants to be a brit!

And QPR are shit!

These great crowds, composed mostly of white working-class men, were evidently fully capable of implicitly lampooning their own prejudices, and those of the British state in refusing citizenship to the Egyptian owner of Harrods, a store in which most of the crowd could not afford to buy much more than a pair of socks. The subtlety and sophistication of the thought of most working-class people when faced by the brutal contradictions which frame our lives is often more considerable, more forgiving, much deeper, and more thoughtful than the judgmentalism of often better educated and more articulate socialists, given to haranguing them from the sidelines.

Of course, not all socialists are as dumb as this, just as not all workers are the saints I'm making them out to be. Generalizations always do violence to the facts; they always contain specific falsehoods amid the general truth one is attempting to get across. For example, most folk are well aware that Benjamin Netanyahu and his ilk are wretched villains, but they do not conclude, as most of the left does, both inside and out of the Labour Party, that Hamas and Hezbollah, or the Palestinian authorities in Ramallah, are any better – they do not support Islamists come what may in the face of Zionism or Zionists, whatever they get up to. The crude attempts at the staging of the morality plays, beloved by the left, in which one side is virtuous and worthy of support, while the other must be condemned to outer darkness, be they Arabs against Jews, Armenians against Azeris, Russians against Ukrainians, or "the rest" against Americans, carry very little weight among the majority of working people. This is because their complicated view of history, and of its contradictions, informs their encounter with the mess and confusion of the world today. Indeed, this is why they know full well that Britain is more peaceful, tolerant, and law-abiding than many "less happier lands."

So too, with a slogan like "I've never kissed a Tory!" Everybody knows that the Conservative Party is replete with bloody selfish buggers capable of riding roughshod over the difficulties experienced by most ordinary working people – schemes like the 5-week waiting time imposed on Universal Credit claimants before they get their hands on any money at all make this plain enough.[6] However, the Tories are a complicated bunch who, broadly speaking, believe that the welfare of everybody in society depends on the prosperity and welfare of businesses and investors. They are often socially liberal, tolerant human beings, capable of as much courtesy and insight as anybody on the left. Depicting Tories, as Labour Party members and the revolutionary left often does, as the Spawn of Satan is absurd and simply indefensible. It leads to a lazy kind of sociology, which often clouds left-wing thought.

Take the attacks on so-called "gentrification." When councils controlled by the Labour Party, in cahoots with property developers and the government, opt for plans designed to change the social character of a neighborhood, by improving public spaces, enhancing house prices, and raising rents, it is common for the left, from Labour Party stalwarts to unruly anarchists, to cry "It's Gentrification!," "Down with Social Cleansing!"[7] As if the people moving into the neighborhood are the problem, rather than the authorities, landowners, and politicians involved. This clearly is an approach congenial to left-wing councils because it directs hostility away from them, toward a much more diffuse entity, "the gentry," whoever they may be. The privatization of public land[8], and the failure to build houses for sale and rent at reasonable prices, is the problem, not the desire of young lower middle-class people to live in nice neighborhoods with good transport links, prosperous ambience, smashing delicatessens, decent bars, and excellent coffee shops. To be sure, some campaigners on the left identify the policies of councils and property developers as the major source of the problem of "gentrification," but a general culture of blame or disapproval by many on the left is attached to the incoming "gentry."

This kind of mis-identification of problems and their causes has calcified in many a left-wing mind in what can only be called snobbery. This snobbery appears to have its origins in old Marxist notions like "false consciousness."[9] The paradox here resides in the way in which many folk on the left associate their outlook and values as intrinsically virtuous, while those who reject or fail to respect the shibboleths of the left are thought either to be wicked, or simply suffering from false consciousness. The latter are clearly thought of as victims of a failure to understand commercial society properly, and therefore need instruction from those endowed with a higher consciousness concerning the cultural hegemony of the bourgeoisie. Snobbery, or a sense of superior taste and understanding, is an inevitable consequence of this ideological frame of mind.

I remember a crude example of this from the early sixties, when I witnessed members of the Communist Party in

Hampstead being hugely amused by a tale concerning the confusion of one of their cleaners, when she was confounded by the unfathomable mysteries of a coffee percolator. This was very direct, and leftist snobbery is often much more subtle, involving disapproval of some kinds of consumption, as opposed to goods and services regarded as more tasteful, healthier, or more aesthetically pleasing than the fast food and kitsch ornaments loved by millions of benighted folk laboring along under the weight of their false consciousness. A consciousness so false that they voted to leave the European Union or doubt the practicality or wisdom of removing immigration controls.

This last point; the vexed question of immigration is usually approached on the left with bad faith or simple denial. The bad faith is represented by expressions of sympathy and support for migrants, while the Labour Party's immigration policy is in substance indistinguishable from that of the Tories. The denial is manifested among those on the left who advocate an open-door policy to the world, saying that everybody is welcome regardless of circumstances. They are on a hiding to nothing, because it is as plain as a pikestaff to the great mass of working men and women that the virtuous left-wingers who argue for open borders have not thought this matter through. Most people wonder at the foolhardiness and naivety of those who spout this nonsense. It's akin to de-funding the police or abolishing the armed forces, it's just plain barmy in its failure to acknowledge the nature of the present conditions.

Such thinking is redolent of the voluntarism and futurity which informs much left-wing thought. The wish is invariably father to thought. Everything from the abolition of nation states, to workers' control of industry is possible because the thought is possible. The fact that demands for workers' control in Britain today exist only among the members of tiny revolutionary groupuscules is surely evidence that workers are not, at this time, seeking to control their workplaces.

These fantastical revolutionary demands have always characterized the insane voluntarism of the left, particularly of Bolshevism and the communist regimes called into being by the "inspiring" Bolshevik initiative in seizing power in Russia in October 1917. Although Bolshevik leaders certainly knew that the vast majority of the population, the peasants, believed in the private ownership of land, the redistribution of aristocratic estates by the communal decision of village councils, and would be resolute opponents of any plan to take their farms and villages from them, the Bolsheviks went ahead regardless. Within a month of taking power Vladimir Lenin, Leon Trotsky, Joseph Stalin, Lev Kamenev, Nikolay Krestinsky, Grigori Sokolnikov, and Andrei Bubnov were ruling by decree, and had founded the *Cheka*, the political police, empowered to imprison and murder opponents at will, without due process, public scrutiny, or formal constraint of any kind.[10]

Ever since, this voluntarism has characterized all communist regimes. There is always a direct administrative solution to any problem. If the peasants oppose collectivization, then we'll deport their community leaders to Central Asia or Siberia, and literally starve millions to death.[11] If we can't secure an alliance with France and Britain, let's do a deal with Hitler.[12] If China needs to create more steel from a standing start then we'll have a "Great Leap Forward" and millions will die.[13] From North Korea to Vietnam and Cambodia, from Havana to Caracas, it's a similar story. Think up the plan, and simply force it through, regardless of the consequences. Bizarrely, this had a strange echo in the politics of the White House that ratified the overthrow of Saddam Hussein in 2003. The ideas of the American Enterprise Institute, and others informing George W. Bush, was to believe that by invading Iraq, removing the Baathists from power, dissolving Iraq's army and state, free enterprise, and democracy would simply arise spontaneously on the ruins. This kind of thinking always results in mayhem and massacres whoever advocates it, whether of the left or the right.

However, although commercial society can boast of a number of examples of this kind of voluntarism, it is invariably the *modus operandi* of the revolutionary left. All are gripped by a vision of the future which apparently legitimates the barbarism of the present. In the Soviet Union this futurity was officially assisted by Socialist Realism that insisted that art should not represent what is, but what is emergent, becoming, going-to-be.[14] This is why amid the poverty and squalor of the Soviet 1930s, artists produced heroic novels, music, and painting, all designed to affirm the line of march dictated by the Communist Party. All works that did not affirm the future in this way were banned, and their creators silenced – killed, imprisoned, exiled – their artworks were simply never allowed to see the light of day.

Fred Kite, the shop steward in the movie *I'm Alright Jack*, exalted this cultural policy with the memorable line: "Ahhh, Russia. All them corn fields, and ballet in the evening."[15] This was a ludicrous joke in 1959 when the film was released, but today it has gained a new lease on life in the "ironic" deployment by young left-wingers of hammer and sickle internet memes, of tee-shirts emblazoned with Soviet iconography, or icons of the sainted killer Che Guavara, and other memorabilia of the "actually existing socialism" of communist party dictatorships. In this way, some on the modern left reveal their preparedness to venerate tyranny and voluntarism, and to embrace misery as a price worth paying for a glorious future. There is, of course, an alternative view that this meme-sharing, particularly among the young, has nothing at all to do with endorsing tyranny, but rather more to do with asserting their own rebellious identity. David Swift recently explained this phenomenon in the following manner:

On the day Fidel Castro died, a gay friend of mine texted me

> to say that he was in an expensive Kings Cross bar, drinking rum and toasting to Fidel. Tedious person that I am I was inclined to text back asking what he felt about Castro's concentration camps for gays, but again this would have been beside the point: young people who ironically venerate tyrants, or who wrap themselves in the colours of Hezbollah and Hamas, aren't oblivious to the crimes committed by the people and organizations; they just don't care. When the young woman put on the Hezbollah t-shirt, she was not making a statement about Israel; she was making a statement about herself. It had nothing to do with the Middle East, and everything to do with the UK.[16]

I doubt that many on the left would take such a benign view of the rough right-wing lads who, for example, adorn themselves with swastikas, even if the flaunting of Nazi symbols forty-odd years ago had rather more to do with punk outrageousness than the Third Reich. However, the wearing of tyrannical symbols, on the right, or the left, is not unconnected with the political outlook of those involved. This is revealed by widespread preparedness on the left to "turn a blind eye" toward the tyrannical or theocratic attitudes of those fighting against Nato and the Western powers, who exhibit a less than resolute commitment to liberal democracy.

Annoyingly, the working class has shown little inclination to follow the left in its, often surreptitious, refusal to defend bourgeois democracy against all comers. Working men and women in Britain have always, in huge majorities, opted for democracy against tyranny of any kind. This, of course, reflects an international reality among workers. For example, nowhere in the world has a communist dictatorship ever been put to the test of a free election. This has been a long-standing practice among the revolutionary left since the Bolsheviks closed down the Constituent Assembly in Petrograd (St Petersburg) in

January 1918, because the Bolsheviks only won a quarter of the seats in the fledgling parliament. Lenin obviously believed in democracy *"in a new way"* and of dictatorship *"in a new way"* – this novelty was occasioned by the "working class" having control of the revolutionary state, and consequently, repressing the bourgeoisie.[17] Lenin thought that by expropriations, seizures, confiscations, and the shootings carried out against the propertied classes, his new state would automatically acquire a proletarian character – i.e. a propertyless character. It would *ipso facto* become the state of the propertyless. In this respect, Russia's revolutionaries proved to be as good as their word, because by 1928 nobody within the Soviet Union had any secure right to any goods, tools, or chattels that they may have to hand.

Trotskyists, and other communists of various hues, insist upon defending this dictatorial tradition by airily talking of the necessary defense of the Revolution, about mythological "workers' control," about the villainous betrayals perpetrated by Stalin, "the bureaucracy," or some other malefactor, or drifting irrelevantly off into meditations about the Soviet defeat of Adolf Hitler, employed by some on the left to this day, to justify the existence of Soviet rule. The only substantial opposition to this on the revolutionary left comes from anarchists and libertarian communists who argue that society should be run by free association, without state forms, or compulsion of any sort; these dreamers are much more in line with the "open-border folk" of today than the dictators, but pursue a politics just as out of touch with the overwhelming majority of working-class people as state-socialist revolutionaries.

In many respects the revolutionary left has more in common with historical re-enactment societies than real political actors, but they do have an uncanny cultural ability to insinuate an outlook toward the achievements of bourgeois democracy – the emancipation of slaves, and the inclusion of the working class into citizenship – which is entirely negative. The achievements of the bourgeoisie, of commercial society, in the defense of private property, and the promotion of free speech, and of government and policing by consent, are said to be as nothing compared to the depredations, exploitation, and inequality sustained by those in charge of commerce, and of our ruling bourgeois oligarchy. Vladimir Lenin famously described freely elected parliaments as merely "a cloak of bourgeois dictatorship," a view which the left, including much of the Labour Party's left, continues to flirt with.

It has recently been argued in some quarters that the capitalist class, the oligarchy that runs commercial society in Britain and throughout the world, has lost confidence in their own system.[18] The evidence for this is the way corporate bosses of giant enterprises, the leaders of key international institutions, and those who provide the public face of the system appear to be bowing down to anti-capitalist elements. As they sit at the feet of Greta Thunberg and the "children's crusade," and carefully note down the pronouncements of the sainted Attenborough; as the human resources departments of big companies assiduously incorporate the edicts issuing from the social justice warriors and identity wallahs on gender and pronouns, or include the latest truths about the intrinsic racism of white workers, discovered by critical race theorists in the universities[19], it is thought that the capitalists have lost their way. Lost their ability to advocate for the virtues of commerce and the kind of life that it gives rise to.

This is to ignore the arguments in which capital's ethical advisors insist that "male, pale, and stale" is bad for the bottom line. The watchwords of ESG – environment, social, governance – are marshaled by bourgeois ideologues to bring the shareholders on-side, in the interests of a healthy return.[20] Those who administer commercial society are well aware that environmental degradation, strife, disorder, and dysfunction are bad for business. Neither should we forget that the social and cultural argument in defense of capitalism has always been the freedom of the individual to define themselves and make their own way in the world. On the face of it, this cardinal virtue of commercial society is being trimmed and cut-about by social justice warriors insisting upon what can be said and thought, but this is only at the turbulent surface of things.

The oligarchy of the rich that runs things knows well that individual liberty and the offer – the prospect, if not the reality – of a life free from poverty and state tyranny is the ace that they hold in their hand against the tyrants in Beijing, or the Erdõgans, the Putins, the Islamists, and the Ayatollahs in Tehran. The capitalist class are undoubtedly under siege from many directions, but their compliance and quiescence in the face of "social justice warriors" and "wokism," are signs, once again, of their seemingly limitless capacity to reinvent themselves culturally and politically, in the service of the way of life over which they rule.

The legitimacy of bourgeois or commercial society is attacked at every level by a concatenation of forces, from the more traditional revolutionaries and socialists on the one hand, to those committed to a species of anti-capitalism that condemns mass consumption and denounces the status of "consumer" among working people on the other. As Costa, a character in Varoufakis's *Another Now*, thinks, "Nothing liberates us from a monopolist more readily than the revelation that we don't want his wares." Costa is informed by what is a perennial trope or theme of leftist thought – commercial society makes us want what we don't need. Apparently, we shouldn't want cars, PlayStation 5, or the latest iPhone. We shouldn't want to stay in good hotels, and fly for vacations in sun-kissed lands. What is clear from this is that the outlook of the neo-Malthusians – the enemies of growth – meets up, in tension, with the traditional moral objections of socialists to the waste and frivolity of commercial society.

We shouldn't want to be consumers, because being consumers in some uncanny way (which is never adequately explained) makes us less free and more alienated from our true selves. It strikes me, and I suspect most of the population, that opposition to having access to a plethora of consumption goods could only arise among people who feel that they already have enough stuff. It really is an upper middle class thought, writ large in the form of an anti-capitalism in tandem with, and closely related to, older socialist objections to advertising, consumption, and commerce, by figures as diverse as Raymond Williams, Tony Benn, George Monbiot, and Zac Goldsmith.

This neo-Malthusianism has arisen in the last 20 years or so and posits the idea that economic growth is unsustainable and must be addressed by reductions in the size of populations and the level of consumption. It's a dismal encounter with capitalism and commerce, intrinsically hostile to the interests of most working people across the globe. The real problem in the world is not that there is too much stuff, but not enough. More than 3 billion people live on less than ten dollars a day, and many millions of working people in a rich state like Britain do not have enough money or possessions to live their lives in a relaxed and purposeful manner. Indeed, the reality and the inability of commercial society to do much to rectify this situation is why capitalism continues to be a problem – it is a society and way of life manifestly capable of creating enough of everything to go around, and yet seems utterly incapable of ensuring that its vast abundance – its cornucopia – spills out to enrich the lives of everybody on the planet.

Now those of us who have always been communists or socialists of one kind or another attribute the key failing or flaw of commercial society to the paradoxical effect of the market system and the profit motive. We know that competition in the market and the drive for profits have historically created and endlessly increased abundance, and tirelessly improved the quality of goods available, and yet it seems that it is the market and the profit motive that renders capitalism incapable of ensuring a more or less equal distribution of goods and services to all.

This is because the market and the profit motive depend entirely upon the institution and security of private property. It was Pierre-Joseph Proudhon who famously denounced "property" as "theft,"[21] but even he did not include the property of peasant farmers, artisans, and small shopkeepers in the theft. The property he had in mind as "theft" was the investment property of big merchants and bankers, of investors, and capitalists in general. The abolition of "bourgeois property" was what Proudhon, and Karl Marx, had in mind when they thought about the acquisition of private property in given historical circumstances. There are also problems, to this day, associated with property and private property which hold great significance to indigenous peoples confronting commercial conceptions of the ownership of land and of access to resources. This brings us perhaps to the most fundamental difference between the majority of working men and women, on one hand, and the socialist and revolutionary left on the other. This difference revolves around respect for private property, and its defense as a matter of law.

The working class has never believed in the abolition or suspension of private property. Even the revolutionary soldiers and sailors at Kronstadt, and the insurgent workers in Petrograd and Moscow repeatedly rose in rebellion against the Bolsheviks when they realized that they'd been hoodwinked – when it dawned on them that there was to be no workers' control, no democracy, and no property a worker or laboring person could call their own. Correspondingly, there was to be no freedom of thought or association either.

There has been extensive discussion of property among philosophers and critics for centuries[22], but it is striking that there has been so little discussion of the problem of private property among socialists throughout recent decades.[23] It may be, of course, that discussions of private property, and the property relations anticipated by socialists, have simply failed to receive much attention, may have gone on below the surface, so to speak. Alternatively, the assumption that the abolition of private property and inheritance are not problematic may well hold sway on the left, as concern about the acquisition of private property by capitalists has always taken center-stage. Often bamboozled by their own theoretical commitments, post-capitalist thinkers, together with those engaged in combined and uneven development studies[24], enjoy speculations which take them to distant realms in which the problem of property scarcely rates a mention. There has also been discussion of participatory economics[25], of co-operation and of cooperatives, of "market socialism" and much else, but little in the way of considering how to disentangle the private property rights of working people from those of the bourgeoisie – how to distinguish the private ownership of consumption goods, including the mortgages, pensions, and savings of workers, from the investment capital held by banks, brokers, and insurance companies.[26]

These lacunae have undoubtedly damaged our ability to engage fully with the working class, the section of commercial society which according to our outlook have the most to gain from socialism. I think we must abandon the notion of false consciousness in its entirety. We must proceed on the assumption that the mass of the people are well acquainted with the commercial, or capitalist mode of life within which they live. They really do not need us to reveal the iniquity of the capitalist system or to bang on about the failings of commercial society. They will only be interested in anything we have to say if we appear to have developed a plausible route out of the contradictions and difficulties inherent in the capitalist system.

This is an extremely tall order. Despite the horror and crime associated with the word and idea of communism, I continue to be a communist, because I continue to believe that democracy should be expanded from the arena of politics, which we now have, to the field of economic life – to the management of the workplace, and the broad direction of economic affairs. I believe that only when investment decisions are truly taken with the welfare of society in mind, first and foremost, will it be possible to tackle the brutal contradiction between plenty on the one hand, and our inability to guarantee universal access to abundance on the other. Consequently, I understand communism to be a utopian project, which could only begin to be realized if the overwhelming majority of the working people actually wanted to dispense with the commercial impulse, and engage instead in the democratic management of economic life.

At the moment there is no prospect of this happening, because the anti-capitalists, the anarchists, the socialists, describe us how you like, have little or no purchase or critical grasp of how we live now, and what exactly it would take to develop a persuasive view of the future capable of engaging the energy and insight of most working men and women. Like most of my comrades on the left, I am often at a loss to know what we should be doing, but I am convinced that whatever it is that we do, it must involve a root and branch rejection by the left of the shibboleths which currently lock us out of real participation in the life of the country, and prevent us from clambering out of the deep trough of irrelevance into which we have fallen.

I am writing this in the midst of the Covid-19 pandemic, and I am deeply conscious that by the time of publication, millions will be unemployed, unable to pay their rent, mortgage, or energy bills, and the desperation and anger of the dispossessed may well have provoked riots and violence on the streets. If nothing else, the widening gulf opening up between the poor and the comfortable will have greatly intensified bitterness, which will doubtless increase as the effects of the Covid-19 economic crisis linger on throughout the years to come. Yet this accumulation of misery will not weaken working people's engagement with commercial society or undermine the widespread belief that inequality is a natural phenomenon. Consequently, I am certain that we socialists, communists, anarchists, and the left more generally must not surrender to the short-termism of running through the streets opposing this or that. We must not continue to make the mistake of thinking that frenzied activism will mask our political bankruptcy. It will not.

It is essential to stop muddling up the prospect of a socialist future with laborism and the potential for "useful reforms." Of course, one should always support useful reforms, but we should not ever be party to spreading the ludicrous idea that such reforms are capable of effecting decisive or fundamental change in the nature or direction of capitalist development. This is because the Labour Party and the trade unions are committed to maintaining commercial society and have never, under any leadership in their history, ever planned to work toward the abolition of capitalism. Socialist aspirations have never been allowed to become muddled up with the party's practical policies. The outlook of Tony Benn in the eighties and Jeremy Corbyn more recently was to inaugurate a decisive shift in the distribution of wealth and power toward working people and their families. Certainly, a laudable objective, but not one that could be achieved without making revolutionary inroads into the ownership and operation of banks, asset managers, and insurance companies. Such moves are inconceivable without the majority of the working class and of the lower middle class on board.

This level of support was never forthcoming for either Benn or Corbyn, consequently both men had always to maintain a fairly large distance between their visceral political desires and their concrete policies. So the Labour Party's left always finds itself stranded uneasily between the ambition of its rhetoric, and the realism of its actual plans and proposals. This is not produced by hypocrisy, but by the recognition among party leaders and activists that the working class is not on board with attacks on private property, or in agreement with cutting the tendons and sinews of commercial society. This accounts for Labour's relentless focus upon welfare, the low paid, and public spending, rather than upon any sharper critique of commerce, or on the inability of capitalism to mobilize its considerable resources for the welfare of the community as a whole, rather than that of the share-holding public.

In this sense, the Labour Party's left-wing faces the same problems as those of us on the far left: the anarchists, communists, and revolutionary socialists. Men and women from the working class, and from the lower middle class, are simply not in favor of handing a blank check to revolutionaries committed to the transformation of society without cast-iron guarantees that their property, their jobs, their freedom, and their way of life will be protected by a radical insurgency, or a revolutionary socialist state. Perhaps, more importantly, they are not persuaded of the need or practicality of workers' control of the businesses that employ them, or of their need to participate in managing the national economy and its international relations.

Our working-class today is not in favor of risking pension funds, mortgages, savings, or our freedom in return for a revolutionary program offered by the left. Working people, all of us, find ourselves embraced by capital, stranded amid a love-hate relationship with the commercial impulse of capitalist society, with its prosperity, vigorous culture, dazzling technology, its poverty, wars, and slumps. We know full-well what its problems are, but we're at a loss to know what to do about them.

Traditionally, the left has banked on the dysfunction of capitalism, of the failure of its "countervailing tendencies," and of the collapse of commerce in a welter of mass unemployment. It is *de rigueur* to talk about "the falling rate of profit," of capitalism being both "late[27]," and crisis ridden. It is sometimes imagined that disintegration is spontaneously embedded into the system. It is often hoped, against all historical evidence to the contrary, that upheaval and economic crisis will improve the prospects of the left. It never has, and probably never will. The economic problems and opportunities of the future undoubtedly reside in the emergence of mass automation, of Artificial Intelligence, and in the merger of bio-tech with info-tech, which are likely to create algorithms which people will learn to trust more readily than their own human judgment.[28] This will be the complete realization of what Karl Marx called the "general intellect" with unfathomable implications for working people in the midst of commercial society. A few years ago, Paul Mason explained it like this:

> [Marx] imagined socially produced information becoming embodied in machines. He imagined this producing a new dynamic, which destroys the old mechanisms for creating prices and profits. He imagined capitalism being forced to develop the intellectual capacities of the worker. And he imagined information coming to be stored and shared in something called the "general intellect" – which was the mind of everybody on earth connected by social knowledge, in which every upgrade benefits everybody. In short, he imagined something close to the info-capitalism in which we live.[29]

Commercial society will not stand still for us; it is a perpetually moving target. Yet the modes of analysis pioneered by Karl Marx in the middle decades of the nineteenth century hold a lesson for us. He struggled to understand capitalist society from the commodity onwards in the most complex manner. He was not always right; his findings were not always borne out by experience, as he fought to understand the social relations that were emerging around him. Yet his commitment to unraveling the mysteries of bourgeois society was always a work in progress, one that had to continue in pace with the world around him. We must do nothing less. It does mean, however, ignoring the injunctions of Frederick Engels and the tradition of refusing to think about the shape and nature of a socialist future. It is true that attempts to inaugurate utopias do not have a good record, and have often resulted in indescribable horror, as revolutionaries have attempted to uproot the present: declaring *Year Zero* in 1975 in Cambodia, or *Year One* in 1792 in Revolutionary France.

The lesson of these catastrophes, and many others, is that those committed to founding a new future must embrace the present, take it with them, so to speak, by not throwing the baby out with the bathwater. They must refuse to squander the accumulated wisdom of any given society, and carefully sort the wheat from the chaff of its laws, jurisprudence, cultural assumptions, and ethical framework. The Emerald City is not our destination, the charlatan behind the curtain is not our guide, and the Yellow Brick Road of traditional socialism will inevitably lead us back, if not to the impoverished farm in Kansas, then to the world we're trying to escape from.[30] Consequently, socialists: moderate and radical; anarchists: bold and fearless; communists: democratic and optimistic need to concentrate on developing a fuller idea of what makes the commercial or capitalist mode of life tick so bloody effectively, if we are ever going to be able to develop and popularize a plausible alternative to the way things are now. The working class will not show the slightest interest in anything we have to say if we fail to map out in detail the road to utopia.

Endnotes

Introduction

1 See Walter Benjamin, *The Arcades Project* (1927-1940), New York: Belknap Press, 2002; and Antonio Gramsci, *Prison Notebooks* (1929-1935), New York: Columbia University Press, 2011.

2 The Annales school of historical scholarship and writing was founded in Strasbourg in 1929 by Marc Bloch and Lucien Febvre; see also the work of English historians Barbara and John Hammond, E. P. Thompson, and Raphael Samuel.

3 Economism comes in a wide variety of forms in which economic activity, or the "base," is thought to determine the shape and nature of all cultural social forms and institutions, often known as the "superstructure." The term economism can also be used by communists of all stripes to describe a species of political opportunism in which the focus of all demands and policies are rooted in economic demands, regarding wages or welfare.

4 See Oscar Wilde's essay *The Soul of Man Under Socialism*, 1891, London: Penguin, 2007.

5 In November 1946 the Communist Party of France won 5.5 million votes (28.26 percent) for the French National Assembly. In 1976 the Italian Communist Party won 34.4 percent in elections for the Italian Parliament.

6 France's communist leader at the outbreak of the Second World War was Maurice Thorez. His wireless broadcasts from Moscow in 1940-1, during the 22 months of the Stalin-Hitler alliance, attacking the British Empire's war with the Third Reich was not the Communist Party of France's finest hour. Much later, in March 1956 the Communist Party of France supported the imposition of emergency powers to crush the independence struggle in Algeria. See

Danièle Simone Joly-Malik, *The French Communist Party and the Algerian War: an ideological turning point?* PhD Thesis, Birmingham: University of Aston, 1982. Later the same year the CPF supported the crushing of the Hungarian Revolution by Soviet troops. A notable exception among communist parties was the Lanka Sama Samaja Party (Lanka Equal Society Party), a Trotskyist organization in Sri Lanka. However, as Trotsky played a leading role in establishing the Bolshevik dictatorship in Russia, it is a moot point to what degree Trotskyist opposition to Stalinism was authentically democratic. The Lanka Equal Society Party was founded in 1935 and became a major political force in the 1940s. At its height in the sixties and seventies it commanded mass support, but it is now a tiny component of a very much larger coalition of the left.

7 See Craig Whitney's article "British Communists Admit Accepting Soviet 'Aid,'" *New York Times*, 15 November, 1991.

Chapter 1

1 Venator Group, formerly the Woolworth Corporation, is the owner of Foot Locker, among many other stores.

2 Patrice Lumumba, the first prime minister of the Republic of Congo, executed by firing squad on 17 January 1961 near Élizabethville, Katanga.

3 *The First Modern Economy: Success, failure, and perseverance of the Dutch economy, 1500 -1815*, by Jan De Vries and Ad Van Der Woude, Cambridge: Cambridge University Press, 1997.

4 See Miles Russell, *Flint mines in Neolithic Britain*, Stroud: Tempus, 2000. There is also evidence of pre-historic copper mining in Llandudno, Wales, dating back three thousand years, and from more than six thousand years ago in Ai Bunar, Bulgaria, and at a number of other ancient sites of varying ages in Serbia, Spain, Austria, and France. Evidently

trade in ore and metals was extensive.

5 R. Bin Wong, "The political economy of agrarian empire and its modern legacy," in Timothy Brook, Gregory Blue (eds.) *China and Historical Capitalism: Genealogies of Sinological Knowledge*, Cambridge: Cambridge University Press, 1999. See also, A. Anievas, K. Nisancioglu, *How the West came to rule the geopolitical origins of capitalism*, London: Pluto, 2015.

6 The distance specified by Pope Alexander VI was 100 leagues.

7 For political developments in England see Steve Pincus, *1688: The first modern revolution*, London: Yale University Press, 2009; for the Netherlands see Maarten Prak, *The Dutch Republic in the Seventeenth Century: The Golden Age*, Cambridge: Cambridge University Press, 2005; see also, Timothy Brook, *Vermeer's Hat: The Seventeenth Century and the Dawn of the Global World*, London: Profile Books, 2008.

8 See E. P. Thompson, *The Making of the English Working Class*, London: Victor Gollancz, 1963. See also Jacques Rancière, *Proletarian Nights: the workers' dream in nineteenth century France*, London: Verso, 2014.

9 For the struggle of farm workers to form a trade union during the 1830s, see Reg Groves, *Sharpen the Sickle! The history of the farm workers' union*, 1949, London: Merlin Press, 2011, pp 13-30. Trade unions were not fully legalized until the Trade Union Act 1871 and the passage of the Conspiracy and Protection of Property Act, 4 years later in 1875.

10 John E. Archer, *Social Unrest and Popular Protest in England, 1780-1840*, Cambridge: Cambridge University Press, 2000; Jacqueline Riding, *Peterloo: the story of the Manchester massacre*, London: Apollo, 2018; Kenneth E. Carpenter (ed.) *The Ten Hours Movement in 1831 and 1832: Six pamphlets and one broadside, 1831-1832*, New York: Arno Press, 1972; Malcolm Chase, *Chartism: a new history*, Manchester: Manchester University Press, 2007; Eric Hobsbawm and George Rudé,

Captain Swing, London: Lawrence and Wishart, 1969.

11 In Britain, following the major democratic reform of 1832 in which middle-class men were enfranchised, the *Municipal Corporations Act* of 1835 empowered local tax payers to run their own town and city councils.

12 Although the Limited Liability Act, which enabled businesses to fail without excessive penalties, was passed in 1855, it was not until 1869 that imprisonment for debt finally ended with the passage of the Bankruptcy Act.

13 See Eric Williams, *Capitalism and Slavery*, Chapel Hill: University of North Carolina Press, 1945.

14 *See* John Aldrich, "The Discovery of Comparative Advantage," *Journal of the History of Economic Thought*, Volume 26, Number 3, September 2004.

15 The Building Societies Act, 1986, permitted building societies to demutualize. The Abbey National Building Society was the first one to become a bank in 1989.

16 For example, Bupa (British United Provident Association) usually returns a healthy profit which is plowed back into private health provision by being reinvested in the business.

17 See the website of the Independent Schools Council, and that of the UK Charity Commission.

18 See the RNLI Annual Report and Accounts, 2019, p.18. See also: https://rnli.org/what-we-do/lifeboats-and-stations/our-lifeboat-stations.

19 See particularly, Jeremy Rifkin, *The Zero Marginal Cost Society: The Internet of things, the collaborative commons, and the eclipse of capitalism*, London: Palgrave Macmillan, 2014; and, Paul Mason, *Postcapitalism: A Guide to Our Future*, London: Allen Lane, 2015.

20 Karl Marx, Frederick Engels, *The Communist Manifesto*, 1848, London: Verso, 1998, pp.38-39.

21 Eric Hobsbawm, "Introduction" to *The Communist Manifesto*, London: Verso,1998, p.17.

Chapter 2

1 "Middle-class values" have, of course, undergone many modifications over the years, but they have remained quintessentially bourgeois values since the inception of commercial society. Daniel Defoe (1660-1731) recounts that the fictional Robinson Crusoe's merchant father said that his social position "was the middle State, or what might be called the upper Station of Low Life, which he had found by long Experience was the best State in the World, the most suited to human Happiness, not exposed to the Miseries and Hardships, the Labour and Sufferings of the mechanic Part of Mankind, and not embarrass'd with the Pride, Luxury, Ambition and Envy of the upper Part of Mankind." Daniel Defoe, *Robinson Crusoe: The Life and Strange Surprising Adventures of Robinson Crusoe* (1719), Oxford: Oxford University Press, 2008.

2 Bert Ramelson, born Baruch Rahmilevich Mendelson, was the full-time secretary of the Communist Party in Leeds when I knew him. He became the party's national industrial organizer in 1965.

3 Wen Zhenheng, *Treatise on Superfluous Things*, circa 1615-1620, published in an English translation by Tony Blishen as *The Elegant Life of the Chinese Literati*, Shanghai: Shanghai Press and Publishing Development, 2019.

4 The "oligarchy" to which I'm referring here is the complex network of connections, friendships, and associations that arose in the British governing class in the aftermath of the great rebellion in India in 1857 that resulted in the consolidation of training for the civil service, and in the systems of promotion and regulation employed in the armed forces, and the management of the empire. There was a hardening of its intrinsically defensive assumptions about race and class, both at home and abroad. It was this oligarchy that began to melt away with the dissolution of

the colonial empire between 1957 and 1967.

5 Following the end of British imperial rule in India (1947) and Burma (1948), only the Crown Colonies, protectorates, and other territories remained in British hands, and these began to become independent, starting with Gold Coast Colony, renamed Ghana, in 1957.

6 Stephen Potter, *Supermanship: Or, how to continue to stay on top without actually falling apart*, Harmondsworth: Penguin, 1958.

7 The British invasion of Egypt prompted by Gamal Abdel Nasser Hussain's unilateral nationalization of the Suez Canal in 1956 was an Anglo-French enterprise in which Israel participated. However, Washington was keen to keep Egypt out of the sphere of Soviet influence at the time, and resolutely opposed the invasion, successfully bringing a rapid end to hostilities.

8 Speech in Bedford, July 20, 1957.

9 Raymond Williams, "Advertising: The Magic System," 1961, in *Problems in Materialism and Culture*, 1980, London: Verso, 1997, pp.185, 190.

10 Stuart Hall, "The Supply of Demand" in E. P. Thompson (ed.) *Out of Apathy*, London: Stevens, 1960. For discussion of the conditions and representations of working-class life during the late fifties and early sixties see Stuart Laing, *Representations of Working Class Life 1957-1964*, Basingstoke: Macmillan, 1986. See also Jeremy Seabrook's discussion of the damage done by rising living standards to the self-confidence and autonomy of working-class people in Jeremy Seabrook's *What Went Wrong: Working People and the Ideals of the Labour Movement*, London, Gollancz, 1978.

11 John Reith was a leading personality of public broadcasting in Britain, and was the Director General of the British Broadcasting Corporation from 1927 to 1938. He was famously concerned with the maintenance, throughout the BBC's output, of a high moral tone and a socially

conservative ethos.

12 The phrase "Public School" in Britain refers to posh fee-paying schools reserved for the children of officers in the armed forces, those of high public officials, well-placed politicians, and the kids of the well-to-do more generally.

13 The Moral Welfare Council of the Church of England produced *The Problem of Homosexuality: An Interim Report*. It was for private circulation and closed discussion, which led to the establishment of the Wolfenden Committee in 1954. The committee published its report in 1957, but its recommendations did not become law until 1967, when sex between two men, over 21 years of age, in private, was finally decriminalized.

14 The average male industrial wage, which for men over 21 was £3-9s-0d (69 Shillings) at the outbreak of the war, had risen to £14-2s-0d (282 Shillings) by 1960. Source: *Hansard*, HC. Deb., 29 November 1960, vol.631 cc42.3W.

15 I'm referring here to the traditional Catholics in the armies of Charles I. Roman Catholics are not usually thought of as religious dissidents, but they were in England in the seventeenth century. See also Ronald Hutton, *The Royalist War Effort 1642-1646*, London: Longman, 1982.

16 See Oscar Wilde's essay *The Soul of Man Under Socialism*, 1891, London: Penguin, 2007.

17 The perils of attempting to determine the size and nature of the middle class by income and consumption rather than occupation and role in the workplace are well discussed by Göran Therborn in "Dreams and Nightmares of the World's middle classes," in *New Left Review*, 127, Second Series, July/August 2020, pp.63-87.

18 Buy-to-let mortgages that will produce a rental income are seen to be an option for some working people who fear that pensions are too expensive or unreliable. Such moves are also a preferred option for observant Muslims seeking ways

around the religious prohibition of interest associated with other kinds of saving.

19 See Antonio Negri and Michael Hardt, *Empire*, Cambridge, Massachusetts: Harvard University Press, 2000. And Michael Hardt and Antonio Negri, *Multitude: War and Democracy in the Age of Empire*, London: Hamish Hamilton, 2005.

20 See Antonio Negri, "Multitude or Working Class" posted on Libcom.org at http://libcom.org/library/multitude-or-working-class-antonio-negri.

21 Even during the struggles in Greece of 2010, it was clear that the sections of the working class mobilizing against the government's austerity measures were disproportionately concentrated in public employment and the government service. On the other hand, large numbers of workers in the private sector were prepared to side with the socialist government and with small proprietors and capitalists in support of budget cuts designed to stabilize the economy. This kind of picture was replicated in the Irish Republic and in a number of other modern economies beset by large government debts and fiscal crisis.

Chapter 3

1 Of course, there is not a sharp temporal distinction between capitalist and pre-capitalist forms of exploitation. Chattel slavery, for example, assumed a new and particularly grotesque form with the development of commercial society. From the beginning of the seventeenth century Africans were shipped, bound hand and foot, to the Americas and the Caribbean to slave on plantations, which were integral to the commercial and industrial development of capitalist society in Europe and North America. See Eric Williams, *Capitalism and Slavery*, Chapel Hill: University of North Carolina Press, 1945; James Walvin, *The Zong: A massacre &*

the end of slavery, New Haven: Yale University Press, 2011; and, C. L. R. James, *The Black Jacobins: Toussaint L'Ouverture and the San Domingo Revolution*, 1936, London: Allison & Busby, 1994.

2 "The many individual capitals invested in a particular branch of production have, with one another, more or less different compositions. The average of their individual compositions gives us the composition of the total capital in this branch of production. Lastly, the average of these averages, in all branches of production, gives us the composition of the total social capital of a country, and with this alone are we, in the last resort, concerned in the following investigation." Karl Marx, *Capital: A Critique of Political Economy*, Vol.1, 1867, London: Lawrence & Wishart, 1983, pp.574-575.

3 I'm indebted to Billy Griffiths for alerting me to the excellent discussion of the production of commodities by "non-commodities," in Nancy Fraser, "Behind Marx's Hidden Abode," *New Left Review*, 86, Spring 2014, pp.55-72.

4 See, Joseph Choonara, "Marx or the Multitude?" *International Socialism*, Issue 105, January 9, 2005.

5 Some people like to refer to national or local taxes as "daylight robbery," but in truth taxes are paid in return for the protection of the social, physical, and industrial infrastructure, and the other services that the state provides; in wealthy democratic capitalist states these imposts are the subject of considerable public debate and scrutiny. They are compulsory, but they are not in any sense, other than the rhetorical, "exploitative."

Chapter 4

1 See Robin DiAngelo, *White Fragility: Why it's so hard for white people to talk about racism*, 2018, London: Penguin, 2019.

2 Seamus Milne, when faced with the choice of schools for his kids, shunned the local comprehensive in preference

for a rather grand grammar school at some distance from their home; Emily Thornberry sent one son to Dame Alice Owen's school and the other to the London Oratory; Shami Chakrabarti sent her son to fee-paying Dulwich College, £18,000 a year; and Diane Abbott sent her son to City of London school, which charges £10,000 a year.

3 See William Morris, *A Dream of John Ball*, and *A King's Lesson*, reprinted from the *Commonweal*, London: Reeves & Turner, 1888.

4 See William Morris, *News from Nowhere, or an Epoch of Rest*, 1890, London: Reeves & Turner, 1894; "Sermon on the Mount," Mathew, Chapters 5, 6, and 7, *English Bible: Authorised Version*, 1611.

5 The slogan *Liberté, Égalité, Fraternité*, although widely associated with the revolution of 1789, did not become the official motto of France until after the establishment of the Third Republic in 1870.

6 For the struggle of the slaves of San Domingo against revolutionary France see C. L. R. James, *The Black Jacobins: Toussaint L'Ouverture and the San Domingo Revolution*, 1936, London: Allison & Busby, 1994.

7 See: Carl J. Richard, *The Louisiana Purchase,* Lafayette: The Center for Louisiana Studies, University of Southwestern Louisiana, 1995, for discussion of the "Louisiana Purchase" of 1803, in which France relinquished all its claims in North America; a great swathe of territory in the Mid-West from what is now southern Alberta; and Saskatchewan in Canada and Montana in the US, down to New Orleans on the Gulf of Mexico.

8 No doubt this skepticism arises from thoughts about Joseph Stalin, the regime of Pol Pot in Kampuchea, the assumption of power by the communists in Beijing in 1949, or Mao Zedong's Cultural Revolution during the years 1966-76.

Chapter 5

1 Timothy Brook, *Vermeer's Hat: The Seventeenth Century and the Dawn of the Global World,* London: Profile Books, 2008, pp.87-95.

2 The *Vereenigde Oostindische Compagnie*; VOC, was founded in 1602.

3 Claude Levi-Strauss "Race and History," in Leo Kuper, ed., *The Race Question in Modern Science,* Paris: Unesco, 1952.

4 George Ritzer, *The McDonaldization of Society,* Los Angeles: Sage, 1993.

5 Activity of this sort was taking place in many parts of the world. For example, the work of Li Shizhen in China resulted in the publication of the *Compendium Materia Medica* (*Ben Cao Gang Mu*) at Nanjing in 1596. This was a vast collection of drawings and information upon herbs with medicinal properties gathered throughout the sixteenth century. However, the worldwide proliferation of such knowledge was largely dependent upon the activity of merchants and seaman engaged in commerce.

6 See Albertus Seba, *Cabinet of Curiosities,* Köln: Taschen, 2003. Albertus Seba's life bridged 2 centuries, from 1665 to 1736. He became an apothecary in Amsterdam which enabled him to collect specimens brought back to the Netherlands by sailors and travelers from all over the globe.

7 The most famous example of this occurred at San Francisco State University in 2016 when Cory Goldstein, a student at SFSU, was berated verbally and physically for "cultural appropriation" because of his dreadlocks. Amusingly, in later interviews, Goldstein made clear his opposition to cultural appropriation in other contexts, just not those which concerned his choice of hairstyle.

8 Henry Jenkins, "Game Design as Narrative Architecture," http://web.mit.edu/~21fms/People/henry3/games&narrative.html, 2001.

9 Fifty years ago there was some discussion of listener participation in the narrative of stories being told to children, if only for research purposes. Alan Dundes, 'Introduction to the Second Edition,' 1968 in Vladimir Propp, *Morphology of the Folktale*, 1927-8, Austin: University of Texas Press, 1968, pp.xi-xvi.

10 I am indebted to Chris Strafford for this observation. See also, Ari Polgar, *Plot, Participation, and Playing Pretend: Narrative Pleasure in Single-Player Video Games*, Middleton: Wesleyan University, 2018.

11 Mark Levine, *The Box: How the Shipping Container made the World Smaller and the World Economy Bigger*, Princeton: Princeton University Press, 2016.

12 Limited liability, and bankruptcy were introduced during the nineteenth century in many jurisdictions in order to replace imprisonment for debt; new laws were enacted to help make the failure and liquidation of companies, and the formation of new enterprises, more fluid, and less onerous to all concerned.

13 In the early 1960s Provident Cheques in the UK were a form of loan, issued by the Provident Financial company, that enabled the borrower to use the check (or voucher) in a variety of different shops to buy whatever one wanted. The "Tallyman" was a door-to-door salesman, who sold goods on credit – he usually visited once a week to collect small payments off the debt, which were rarely ever paid off because customers were regularly encouraged to take yet more goods on credit – it was buying on "the never-never."

Chapter 6

1 For the "Glorious Revolution," which established constitutional monarchy and the supremacy of parliament in England, see Steve Pincus, *1688: The First Modern Revolution*, New Haven: Yale University Press, 2009.

2 E. P. Thompson, "Eighteenth-century English society: class struggle without class?" *Social History*, Volume 3, Number 2, May 1978, pp.133-165.

3 See John A. Phillips, "The Structure of Electoral Politics in Unreformed England," *Journal of British Studies*, Volume 19, Number 1 (Autumn 1975), Cambridge: Cambridge University Press, pp.l75-100.

4 The Kingdom of Ireland was a fictional realm dreamed up in the sixteenth century by England's rulers, with its own parliament in Dublin until the "Irish" monarchy was merged with that of England and Scotland, creating the United Kingdom of Great Britain and Ireland in 1801.

5 A campaign for universal suffrage, which at the time meant votes for all men, regardless of income or property, was initiated as early as 1792 by the London Corresponding Society. In the same year, Mary Wollstonecraft published the *Vindication of the Rights of Women*, but the battle for women's suffrage did not begin in earnest until 1848-1850.

6 See George Eliot's novel *Felix Holt, The Radical*, 1866, London: Penguin, 1995.

7 The Irish Republican Brotherhood was founded around 1858, and was dedicated to the overthrow of British rule in Ireland. See Owen McGee, *The IRB: The Irish Republican Brotherhood from The Land League to Sinn Féin*, Dublin: Four Courts Press, 2005. For a flavor of the time see T. D. Sullivan, *The Dock and the Scaffold: The Manchester Tragedy and the Cruise of the Jacknell*, 1868, Dublin: Leopold Classic Library, 2015.

8 See Eric Williams, *Capitalism and Slavery*, Chapel Hill: University of North Carolina Press, 1945.

9 This fear of adverse Divine Judgement was greatly intensified when Olaudah Equiano alerted anti-slavery campaigners to the Zong Massacre in which more than 130 Africans were thrown overboard as "cargo" from the slave

ship Zong in November 1781. See James Walvin, *The Zong: A massacre & the end of slavery*, New Haven: Yale University Press, 2011.

10 See Sir Robert Peel's 9 Principles of Policing, 1829 – published as "Definition of Policing by Consent," Home Office, www.gov.uk, 2012. See also Jonathan Jackson, et. al., "Compliance with the law and policing by consent: notes on police and legal legitimacy," in Adam Crawford, Anthea Hucklesby (eds.) *Legitimacy and Compliance in Criminal Justice*, London: Routledge, 2012.

11 See discussion of the cholera epidemic of 1831-2 in E. Ashworth Underwood, "The History of Cholera in Britain," *Proceedings of the Royal Society of Medicine*, Volume XVI, November 3, 1947.

12 See Kenan Malik, *Multiculturalism and Its Discontents: Rethinking Diversity After 9/11*, London: Seagull Books, 2013.

13 See John Nelson Tarn, *Five Per Cent Philanthropy: an account of housing in urban areas between 1840 and 1914*, Cambridge: Cambridge University Press, 1973; See also Luke Samy, "The Building Society Promise: Building Societies and Home Ownership, circa 1880 to 1913," *University of Oxford Discussion Papers in Economic and Social History*, Number 72, Oxford: Oxford University, 2008; and, Martin J. Daunton, *House and home in the Victorian city: working class housing 1850-1914*, London: Edward Arnold, 1983.

14 Frederick Engels, *The Housing Question*, 1872-1873, London: Union Books, 2012.

15 Cited by Samuel Smiles in the *Building Societies Gazette*, General Reference Collection British Library, 1879, p.55; G. J. Holyoake, *The History of Co-operation in England: Its Literature and Advocates*, published in London, 1875-1877.

16 Cited in Michael Cassell, *Inside Nationwide: One Hundred Years of Co-operation*, London: Nationwide Building Society, 1984.

17 The Nigerian lad, Damilola Taylor, was ten in 2000 when his artery was severed in a knife attack in Peckham, and he died in the stairwell of a block of flats. It took three trials over 6 years before anyone was convicted of the killing.

18 Black British teenager Stephen Lawrence was killed while waiting at a bus stop in Eltham by a gang of racists in April 1993. There was a long struggle to secure convictions, dragging on for many years, years which also involved high-profile investigations of police conduct.

19 See Davide Consoli, *The evolution of retail banking services in United Kingdom: a retrospective analysis*, Working Paper 13, Manchester: Centre for Research on Innovation & Competition, 2003.

20 https://www.raisin.co.uk/newsroom/articles/better-saving-money/.

Chapter 7

1 Tony Cliff, *The Employers' Offensive: Productivity deals and how to fight them*, London: Pluto Press, 1970.

2 The Socialist Review Group, founded in 1950, became the International Socialists in 1962, and subsequently became the Socialist Workers Party in 1977.

3 Don Milligan, *The Politics of Homosexuality*, London: Pluto Press, 1973. Full text available at www.donmilligan.net, Articles, 1973.

4 Everybody employed in the production of newspapers on Fleet Street had to be a member of their appropriate union. The National Graphical Association (NGA), the Society of Graphical and Allied Trades (SOGAT), and the Amalgamated Union of Engineering Workers (AUEW) all maintained *closed shops*, effectively determining who was hired and who was not.

5 See, Trade Union Congress, at https://tuc150.tuc.org.uk/stories/the-wapping-dispute/.

6 See the preface of Karl Marx's *A Contribution to the Critique of Political Economy*, where he stresses that, "It is not the consciousness of men that determines their existence, but their social existence that determines their consciousness." "Preface," *A Contribution to the Critique of Political Economy*, 1859, *Karl Marx and Frederick Engels: Selected Works in one volume*, London: Lawrence & Wishart, 1968, p.181.

7 E. P. Thompson, *The Making of the English Working Class*, London: Victor Gollancz, 1963.

8 Office for National Statistics, July 2014, https://www.ons.gov.uk/peoplepopulationandcommunity/birthsdeathsandmarriages/marriagecohabitationandcivilpartnerships/articles/whatdoesthe2011censustellusaboutinterethnicrelationships/2014-07-03.

9 Kully Kaur-Ballagan, *Attitudes to race and inequality in Britain*, London: Ipsos MORI, 5-10 June, 2020.

10 Steps made toward the material independence of women from their husbands began to be taken with the passage of the Married Women's Property Act, 1870, and the Married Women's Property Act of 1882. These laws, taken together, finally established that a wife and her husband were entirely separate and independent legal persons, and overturned the idea that the wife was, on marriage, legally subsumed into the person of her husband.

11 For reflection on the oppression of homosexuals, see particularly Matt Cook, *London and the culture of homosexuality, 1885-1914*, Cambridge: Cambridge University Press, 2003; and Helen Smith, *Masculinity, Class and Same-Sex Desire in Industrial England, 1895-1957*, Basingstoke: Palgrave Macmillan, 2015.

12 See Geoffrey Evans, Jonathan Mellon, "Social Class" in John Curtice, et. al., *British Social Attitudes 33rd Report*, London: The National Centre for Social Research, 2016. See also John Curtice, Ian Simpson, "Voting" in D. Phillips, et. al., *British*

Social Attitudes 35th Report, London: The National Centre for Social Research, 2018.

Conclusion

1 Mark Fisher, *Capitalist Realism: Is there no alternative?* Winchester: Zero Books, 2009. For a discussion of Fredric Jameson's use of the thought that, "It is easier to imagine the end of the world than the end of capitalism," see Matthew Beaumont, "Imagining the End Times: Ideology, the Contemporary Disaster Movie, *Contagion*," in Matthew Flisfeder, Louis-Paul Willis (eds.) *Žižek and Media Studies*, Basingstoke: Palgrave Macmillan, 2014.

2 Marx makes a similar point in his *Critique of the Gotha Programme*: "What we have to deal with here is a communist society, not as it has *developed* on its own foundations, but, on the contrary, just as it *emerges* from capitalist society; which is thus in every respect, economically, morally and intellectually, still stamped with the birth marks of the old society from whose womb it emerges," Karl Marx, *Critique of the Gotha Programme*, 1875, Peking: Foreign Languages Press, 1972, p.15.

3 Yanis Varoufakis, *Another Now: Dispatches from an Alternative Present*, London: The Bodley Head, 2020.

4 William Morris, *News from Nowhere*, 1890, London: Longmans, Green & Co., 1899.

5 The exception to this, of course, is the Saltire, the ancient flag of Scotland, much waved by supporters of the campaign for Scotland's independence from the United Kingdom. However, there is not much flag waving in England, Wales, or Northern Ireland, beyond that involved in football competitions.

6 You can ask for an emergency payment while you're waiting for your regular payments to commence, but there is no guarantee that you'll get the emergency money you ask for,

because they are discretionary payments.

7 See "Fight for the City: Social Cleansing, Social Warfare," *Organise!* No.84, London: Anarchist Federation, Summer, 2015.

8 See Brett Christophers, *The New Enclosure: The Appropriation of Public Land in Neoliberal Britain*, London: Verso, 2018.

9 "False consciousness" is an expression that arose with Frederick Engels in the 1890s, and was deployed throughout the twentieth century by many Marxists who attempted, with considerable sophistication, to develop a way of thinking about how people misunderstand the nature of class relations within capitalist society. See, Ron Eyerman, "False Consciousness and Ideology in Marxist Theory," *Acta Sociologica*, Volume 24, Number 1/2, Work and Ideology, 1981, pp.43-56.

10 See Don Milligan, *October 1917: An intoxication with the future*, Articles, November 3, 2017, www.donmilligan.net; and Don Milligan, *Stalinism, Tradition, and the Working Class: A response to comrades who honeymoon in the past*, Articles, May 11, 2015, www.donmilligan.net.

11 Anne Applebaum, *Red Famine: Stalin's War on Ukraine*, London: Allen Lane, 2017.

12 Roger Moorhouse, *The Devils' Alliance: Hitler's Pact with Stalin 1939-1941*, London: The Bodley Head, 2014.

13 Frank Dikötter, *Mao's Great Famine: The history of China's most devastating catastrophe, 1958-62*, London: Bloomsbury, 2010.

14 See Katerina Clark, (1981) *The Soviet Novel: History as Ritual*, Bloomington and Indianapolis: Indiana University Press, 2000. See also Nicolai Bukharin, (1934) "Poetry, Poetics and the Problems of Poetry in the USSR" in H. G. Scott (ed.) *Soviet Writers' Congress 1934: The Debate on Socialist Realism and Modernism*, London: Lawrence & Wishart, 1977.

15 *I'm All Right Jack* was a British film, released in 1959, in

which the left-wing shop steward, Fred Kite, played by Peter Sellers, is lampooned for his naïve enthusiasm for socialist realism and Soviet reality.

16 David Swift, *A Left for Itself: Left-wing Hobbyists and Performative Radicalism,* Winchester: Zero Books, 2019, p.130.

17 V. I. Lenin, *The State and Revolution,* 1918, Peking: Foreign Languages Press, 1976, pp.41-43.

18 See James Heartfield, "Capitalism and Anti-Capitalism," in *Interventions* Volume 5(2), 2993, pp.271-289; See also Frank Füredi, "The birth of the culture wars," *Spiked-online,* 19 June 2020.

19 Kimberlé Crenshaw et. al., (eds.) *Critical race theory: the key writings that formed the movement,* New York: New Press, 1995. For counter arguments see Andrew Murray, *The Madness of Crowds: Gender, Race, Identity,* London: Bloomsbury Continuum, 2019.

20 I am indebted to the "bourgeois ideologue," James Jarvis, for this observation. James is a friend, and former student of mine, who, despite our numerous disagreements, has always startled me with the sharpness of his political insights.

21 See, Pierre-Joseph Proudhon, *What is Property? Or, an Inquiry into the Principle of Right and of Government,* 1840, London: William Reeves, 1969.

22 See Jeremy Waldron, "What is Private Property," *Oxford Journal of Legal Studies,* Volume 5, Number 3, Oxford: Oxford University Press, 1985. See also the *Stanford Encyclopedia of Philosophy* entry on property at https://plato.stanford.edu/entries/property/.

23 There has, of course, been some discussion of this question over the years. See John Spargo, "Private Property and Personal Liberty in the Socialist State," *North American Review,* June 1909, Volume 189, Number 643, pp.844-856; See Andrew Kernohan, "Democratic Socialism and Private

Property," *Studies in Political Economy*, 22, Spring 1987, London: Routledge; See also Patrick Flaherty, "Recasting the Soviet State: Organizational Politics in the Gorbachev Era," *Socialist Register: Problems of Socialist Renewal, East & West*, Vol. 24, 1988.

24 See Luke Cooper, "Worlds beyond capitalism: images of uneven and combined development" in Kim Stanley Robinson's *Mars trilogy, Cambridge Review of International Affairs*, Cambridge: Routledge, 2020.

25 See Albert Michael and Robin Hahnel, *The Political Economy of Participatory Economics,* Princeton: Princeton University Press, 1991; See also Albert Michael, *Parecon: Life after capitalism*, London: Verso, 2003.

26 For an ordinary evasion of the difficulties inherent in distinguishing between "capital" and "consumption goods," see Marx Memorial Library, "Is private property peculiar to capitalism and do socialists want to abolish it?" London: *Morning Star on-line*, April 23, 2017.

27 See particularly, Ernst Mandel, *Late Capitalism*, 1972, London: Verso, 1999; Also Fredric Jameson, "Postmodernism: or, the Cultural Logic of Late Capitalism," 1984, in Fredric Jameson, *Postmodernism: or, the Cultural Logic of Late Capitalism* London: Verso, 1991.

28 See Yuval Noah Harari, *Homo Deus: A Brief History of Tomorrow*, New York: HarperCollins, 2017.

29 Paul Mason, *Postcapitalism: A guide to our future*, London: Allen Lane, 2015. See also: Carlo Vercellone, "From Formal Subsumption to General Intellect: Elements for a Marxist Reading of the Thesis of Cognitive Capitalism," *Historical Materialism 15*, 2007, pp.13-36.

30 See Frank Baum, *The Wonderful Wizard of Oz*, London Penguin, 1998; Originally published in Chicago by George M. Hill Company in 1900. See also the movie, *The Wizard of Oz*, released by Metro-Goldwyn-Mayer, 1939.

Bibliography

ALDRICH, John, "The Discovery of Comparative Advantage," *Journal of the History of Economic Thought,* Volume 26, Number 3, September 2004.

ANGLICAN clergy and doctors, etc., *The Problem of Homosexuality: An Interim Report,* London: Church of England, Church Information Board, 1954.

ANIEVAS, A. and NISANCIOGLU, K., *How the West came to rule the geopolitical origins of capitalism,* London: Pluto, 2015.

APPLEBAUM, Anne, *Red Famine: Stalin's War on Ukraine,* London: Allen Lane, 2017.

APPLEBY, Joyce, *The Relentless Revolution: A History of Capitalism,* New York: W. W. Norton & Company, 2010.

ARCHER, John E., *Social Unrest and Popular Protest in England, 1780-1840,* Cambridge: Cambridge University Press, 2000.

ASHWORTH UNDERWOOD, E., "The History of Cholera in Britain," *Proceedings of the Royal Society of Medicine,* Volume XVI, November 3, 1947.

BANAJI, Jairus, *Agrarian Change in Late Antiquity: Gold, Labour, and Aristocratic Dominance,* Oxford: Oxford University Press, 2001.

BANAJI, Jairus, *Theory as History: Essays on Modes of Production and Exploitation,* Leiden: Brill, 2010.

BANERJEE, Abhijit V., and DUFLO, Ester, *Poor Economics: A Radical Rethinking of the Way to Fight Global Poverty,* New York: Public Affairs, 2011.

BAUM, Frank, *The Wonderful Wizard of Oz,* 1900, London Penguin, 1998.

BEAUMONT, Matthew, "Imagining the End Times: Ideology, the Contemporary Disaster Movie, *Contagion,*" in Matthew Flisfeder and Louis-Paul Willis, (eds.) *Žižek and Media Studies,* Basingstoke: Palgrave Macmillan, 2014.

BENGRY, Justin, "Class and Same-Sex Desire in Industrial England, 1895-1957," *Social History*, Volume 42, Number 1, 2017, pp.143-145.

BENJAMIN, Walter, *The Arcades Project*, 1927-1940, New York: Belknap Press, 2002.

BERNSTEIN, William J., *The Birth of Plenty: How the Prosperity of the Modern World Was Created*, New York: McGraw-Hill, 2004.

BIN WONG, R., "The political economy of agrarian empire and its modern legacy," in Timothy Brook and Gregory Blue (eds.) *China and Historical Capitalism: Genealogies of Sinological Knowledge*, Cambridge: Cambridge University Press, 1999.

BLOCH, Marc, *Feudal Society*, 1939, New York: Routledge, 2014.

BRASS, Tom, *Towards a Comparative Political Economy of Unfree Labour: Case Studies and Debates*, London: Taylor & Francis, 1999.

- (2005) "Late Antiquity as Early Capitalism?" *The Journal of Peasant Studies*, Volume 32. Number 1, 2005, pp.118-150.

- (2011) *Labour Regime Change in the Twenty-First Century: Unfreedom, Capitalism and Primitive Accumulation*, Chicago: Haymarket Books, 2011.

BRAUDEL, Fernand, *Capitalism and Material Life*, translated from *Civilisation matérielle et capitalisme*, 1967, by Miriam Kochan, London: Weidenfeld and Nicolson, 1973.

BROOK, Timothy, BLUE, Gregory (eds.) *China and Historical Capitalism: Genealogies of Sinological Knowledge*, Cambridge: Cambridge University Press, 1999.

BROOK, Timothy, *Vermeer's Hat: The Seventeenth Century and the Dawn of the Global World*, London: Profile Books, 2008.

BROWN, Gordon, *Beyond the Crash: Overcoming the First Crisis of Globalisation*, London: Simon & Schuster, 2010.

BUKHARIN, Nicolai, "Poetry, Poetics and the Problems of Poetry in the USSR," 1934, in H. G. Scott (ed.) *Soviet Writers' Congress 1934: The Debate on Socialist Realism and Modernism*, London: Lawrence & Wishart, 1977.

CARPENTER, Kenneth E., (ed.) *Ten Hours Movement in 1831 and 1832: Six pamphlets and one broadside, 1831-1832*, New York: Arno Press, 1972.

CASSELL, Michael, *Inside Nationwide: One Hundred Years of Co-operation*, London: Nationwide Building Society, 1984.

CHANG, Ha-Joon, *23 Things They Don't Tell You About Capitalism*, London: Allen Lane, 2010.

CHASE, Malcolm, *Chartism: a new history*, Manchester: Manchester University Press, 2007.

CHOONARA, Joseph, "Marx or the Multitude?" *International Socialism*, Issue 105, January 9, 2005.

CHRISTOPHERS, Brett, *The New Enclosure: The Appropriation of Public Land in Neoliberal Britain*, London: Verso, 2018.

CLARK, Katerina, *The Soviet Novel: History as Ritual*, 1981, Bloomington and Indianapolis: Indiana University Press, 2000.

CLIFF, Tony, *The Employers' Offensive: Productivity deals and how to fight them*, London: Pluto Press, 1970.

COHEN, G. A., *Karl Marx's Theory of History: A Defence*, 1978, Oxford: Clarendon Press, 2004.

CONSOLI, Davide, *The evolution of retail banking services in United Kingdom: a retrospective analysis*, Working Paper 13, Manchester: Centre for Research on Innovation & Competition, 2003.

COOK, Matt, *London and the culture of homosexuality, 1885-1914*, Cambridge: Cambridge University Press, 2003.

COOPER, Luke, "Worlds beyond capitalism: images of uneven and combined development," in Kim Stanley Robinson's *Mars trilogy, Cambridge Review of International Affairs*, Cambridge: Routledge, 2020.

CRENSHAW, Kimberlé, et. al., (eds.) *Critical race theory: the key writings that formed the movement*, New York: New Press, 1995.

CURTICE, John and SIMPSON, Ian, "Voting" in D. Phillips, et. al., *British Social Attitudes 35th Report*, London: The National

Centre for Social Research, 2018.

DAUNTON, Martin J., *House and home in the Victorian city: working class housing 1850-1914*, London: Edward Arnold, 1983.

DEFOE, Daniel, *Robinson Crusoe: The Life and Strange Surprising Adventures of Robinson Crusoe,* 1719, Oxford: Oxford University Press, 2008.

DiANGELO, Robin, *White Fragility: Why it's so hard for white people to talk about racism*, 2018, London: Penguin, 2019.

DIKÖTTER Frank, *Mao's Great Famine: The history of China's most devastating catastrophe, 1958-62*, London: Bloomsbury, 2010.

DOBB, Maurice, *Studies in the Development of Capitalism*, 1946, London: Routledge and Kegan Paul, 1963.

— (1967) *Papers on Capitalism, Development and Planning,* London: Routledge and Kegan Paul, 1967.

DUNDES, Alan, "Introduction to the Second Edition," 1968, in Vladimir Propp, *Morphology of the Folktale*, 1927-8, Austin: University of Texas Press, 1968.

ELIOT, George, *Felix Holt, The Radical*, 1866, London: Penguin, 1995.

ENGELS, Frederick, "The Housing Question," *Volksstaat*, Leipzig, 1872-1873, London: Union Books, 2012.

EVANS, Geoffrey, MELLON, Jonathan, "Social Class" in John Curtice, et. al., *British Social Attitudes 33rd Report*, London: The National Centre for Social Research, 2016.

EYERMAN. Ron, "False Consciousness and Ideology in Marxist Theory," *Acta Sociologica*, Volume 24, Number 1/2, Work and Ideology, 1981, pp.43-56.

FISHER, Mark, *Capitalist Realism: Is there no alternative?* Winchester: Zero Books, 2009.

FLAHERTY, Patrick, "Recasting the Soviet State: Organizational Politics in the Gorbachev Era," *Socialist Register: Problems of Socialist Renewal, East & West*, Volume 24, 1988.

FRASER, Nancy, "Behind Marx's Hidden Abode," *New Left*

Review, 86, Spring 2014, pp.55-72.

FUKUYAMA, Francis, *The Origins of Political Order,* London: Profile Books, 2011.

FÜREDI Frank, "The birth of the culture wars," *Spiked-online,* 19 June 2020.

GOLDTHWAITE, Richard A., *The Economy of Renaissance Florence,* Baltimore: John Hopkins University Press, 2009.

GRAMSCI, Antonio, *Prison Notebooks,* 1929-1935, New York, Columbia University Press, 2011.

GROVES, Reg, *Sharpen the Sickle! The history of the farm workers' union,* 1949, London: Merlin Press, 2011.

HACKER, Jacob S., and PIERSON, Paul, *Winner-Take-All Politics: How Washington Made the Rich Richer and Turned Its Back on the Middle Class,* New York: Simon & Schuster, 2010.

HALL, Stuart, "The Supply of Demand" in E. P. Thompson (ed.) *Out of Apathy,* London: Stevens, 1960.

HAMMOND, Barbara, HAMMOND, John, *The Town Labourer, 1760-1832: The new civilization*, London: Longmans, Green, & Co., 1925.

HARARI, Yuval Noah, *Sapiens: A Brief History of Humankind,* 2011, London: Vintage, 2015.

— (2017) *Homo Deus: A Brief History of Tomorrow,* New York: HarperCollins, 2017.

HEARTFIELD, James, "Capitalism and Anti-Capitalism," in *Interventions* Volume 5(2), 2003.

HOBSBAWM, Eric, and RUDÉ, George, *Captain Swing,* London: Lawrence and Wishart, 1969.

HOBSBAWM, Eric, "Introduction" to Karl Marx, Frederick Engels, *The Communist Manifesto: Modern Edition,* London: Verso, 1998.

HOLYOAKE, G. J., *The History of Co-operation in England: Its Literature and Advocates,* published in London, 1875-1877.

HUTTON, Ronald, *The Royalist War Effort 1642-1646,* London: Longman, 1982.

JACKSON, Jonathan, et. al., "Compliance with the law and policing by consent: notes on police and legal legitimacy," in Adam Crawford, Anthea Hucklesby (eds.) *Legitimacy and Compliance in Criminal Justice*, pp.29-49, London: Routledge, 2012.

JAMES, C. L. R., *The Black Jacobins: Toussaint L'Ouverture and the San Domingo Revolution*, 1936, London: Allison & Busby, 1994.

JAMESON, Fredric, "Postmodernism: or, the Cultural Logic of Late Capitalism," 1984, in Fredric Jameson, *Postmodernism: or, the Cultural Logic of Late Capitalism*, London: Verso, 1991.

JENKINS Henry, "Game Design as Narrative Architecture," *http://web.mit.edu/~21fms/People/henry3/games&narrative.html*, 2001.

JOLY-MALIK, Danièle Simone, *The French Communist Party and the Algerian War: an ideological turning point?* PhD Thesis, Birmingham: University of Aston, 1982.

KALETSKY, Anatole, *Capitalism 4.0: The Birth of a New Economy*, London: Bloomsbury, 2010.

KAUR-BALLAGAN, Kully, *Attitudes to race and inequality in Britain*, London: Ipsos MORI, 5-10, June, 2020.

KEMP, Jessica McKelvie, "Soliciting desire: the ad-man as narrative negotiation between art, desire, and consumer capitalism in twentieth-century novels," Baton Rouge: Louisiana State University, Doctoral Dissertations, 2007.

KERNOHAN, Andrew, "Democratic Socialism and Private Property," *Studies in Political Economy*, 22, Spring 1987, London: Routledge, 1987.

LAING, Stuart, *Representations of Working Class Life 1957-1964*, Basingstoke: Macmillan, 1986.

LAZZARATO, Maurizio, *The Making of the Indebted Man*, Los Angeles: Semiotext(e) Series 13, 2012.

LEBVRE, Lucien, *The Problem of Unbelief in the Sixteenth Century: The Religion of Rabelais*, 1937, London: Harvard University

Press, 1982.

LENIN, V. I., *The State and Revolution*, 1918, Peking: Foreign Languages Press, 1976.

LEVINE, Mark, *The Box: How the Shipping Container made the World Smaller and the World Economy Bigger*, Princeton: Princeton University Press, 2016.

LEVI-STRAUSS, Claude "Race and History," in Leo Kuper (ed.) *Race and History: The Race Question in Modern Science*, Paris: Unesco, 1952.

LEWIS, Michael, *The Big Short, A True Story*, 2010, London: Penguin Books, 2011.

McGEE, Owen, *The IRB: The Irish Republican Brotherhood from The Land League to Sinn Féin*, Dublin: Four Courts Press, 2005.

MALIK, Kenan, *Multiculturalism and Its Discontents: Rethinking Diversity After 9/11*, London: Seagull Books, 2013.

MANDEL, Ernst, *Late Capitalism*, 1972, London: Verso, 1999.

MARX, Karl, "Preface," *A Contribution to the Critique of Political Economy*, 1859, *Karl Marx and Frederick Engels: Selected Works in one volume*, London: Lawrence & Wishart, 1968.

— (1867) *Capital: A Critique of Political Economy*, Volume I, reproduced from the English edition of 1887, London: Lawrence & Wishart, 1983.

— (1875) *Critique of the Gotha Programme*, Peking: Foreign Languages Press, 1972.

MARX, Karl and ENGELS, Frederick, *The Manifesto of the Communist Party*, 1848, (this translation first published in 1888), in *The Communist Manifesto: Modern Edition* introduced by Eric Hobsbawm, London: Verso, 1998.

MARX Memorial Library, "Is private property peculiar to capitalism and do socialists want to abolish it?" London: *Morning Star on-line*, April 23, 2017.

MASON, Paul, *Postcapitalism: A Guide to Our Future*, London: Allen Lane, 2015.

MICHAEL, Albert, HAHNEL, Robin, *The Political Economy*

of Participatory Economics, Princeton: Princeton University Press, 1991.

MICHAEL Albert, *Parecon: Life after capitalism,* London: Verso, 2003.

MILLIGAN, Don, *The Politics of Homosexuality,* London: Pluto Press, 1973.

(2003) *The Aesthetic of Emancipation: A study of the relation between Raymond Williams's socialism and his literary criticism, cultural analysis and theoretical writings,* PhD Thesis, Milton Keynes: Open University.

— (2015) *Stalinism, Tradition, and the Working Class: A response to comrades who honeymoon in the past,* Manchester: Articles May 11, 2015, www.donmilligan.net.

— (2017) *October 1917: An intoxication with the future,* Manchester: Articles, November 3, 2017, www.donmilligan.net.

MOORHOUSE, Roger, *The Devils' Alliance: Hitler's Pact with Stalin 1939-1941,* London: The Bodley Head, 2014.

MORRIS, William, *A Dream of John Ball,* and *A King's Lesson,* reprinted from the *Commonweal,* 1886, London: Reeves & Turner, 1888.

— (1890) *News from Nowhere, or an Epoch of Rest,* London: Longmans, Green & Co., 1899.

MURRAY, Andrew, *The Madness of Crowds: Gender, Race, Identity,* London: Bloomsbury Continuum, 2019.

NEGRI Antonio, "Multitude or Working Class," Contribution to a debate at the European Social Forum in Paris, 2003, posted in 2006 at Libcom.org.

NEGRI, Antonio and HARDT, Michael, 2000, *Empire,* Cambridge, Massachusetts: Harvard University Press, 2000.

— (2005) *Multitude: War and Democracy in the Age of Empire,* London: Hamish Hamilton, 2005,

PINCUS, Steve, *1688: The first modern revolution,* by Steve Pincus, London: Yale University Press, 2009.

POLGAR, Ari, *Plot, Participation, and Playing Pretend: Narrative*

Pleasure in Single-Player Video Games, BA Thesis, Middleton: Wesleyan University, 2018.

POTTER, Stephen, *Supermanship: Or, how to continue to stay on top without actually falling apart,* Harmondsworth: Penguin, 1958.

PRAK, Maarten, *The Dutch Republic in the Seventeenth Century: The Golden Age,* Cambridge: Cambridge University Press, 2005.

PROUDHON, Pierre-Joseph, *What is Property? Or, an Inquiry into the Principle of Right and of Government,* 1840, London: William Reeves, 1969.

RANCIÈRE, Jacques, *Proletarian Nights: The Workers' Dream in Nineteenth Century France,* 1981, London: Verso, 2012.

RICARDO, David, *On the Principles of Political Economy and Taxation,* 1817, Library of Economics and Liberty: https://www.econlib.org/library/Ricardo/ricP.html?chapter_num=1#book-reader, 1999.

RICHARD, Carl J., *The Louisiana Purchase,* Lafayette: The Center for Louisiana Studies, University of Southwestern Louisiana, 1995.

RIDING, Jacqueline, *Peterloo: the story of the Manchester massacre,* London: Apollo, 2018.

RIFKIN, Jeremy, *The Zero Marginal Cost Society: The Internet of things, the collaborative commons, and the eclipse of capitalism,* London: Palgrave Macmillan, 2014.

RITZER George, *The McDonaldization of Society,* Los Angeles: Sage, 1993.

ROSEN, William, *The Most Powerful Idea in the World: A Story of Steam, Industry and Invention,* London: Jonathan Cape, 2010.

RUSSELL, Miles, *Flint mines in Neolithic Britain,* Stroud: Tempus, 2000.

SAMUELS, Raphael, (ed.) *Village life and labour,* London: Routledge and Kegan Paul. 1975.

SAMY, Luke, "The Building Society Promise: Building Societies and Home Ownership, circa 1880 to 1913," in *University of Oxford Discussion Papers in Economic and Social History*, Number 72, Oxford: Oxford University, 2008.

SEABROOK, Jeremy, *What Went Wrong: Working People and the Ideals of the Labour Movement*, London, Gollancz, 1978.

SEBA, Albertus, *Cabinet of Curiosities*, Köln: Taschen, 2003.

SEN, Amartya, *The Idea of Justice*, 2009, London: Penguin, 2010.

SMITH, Adam, *The Theory of Moral Sentiments*, 1759, Jonathan Bennett: Early Modern Texts, 2008, www.earlymoderntexts.com, 2017.

— (1776) *An Inquiry into the Nature and Causes of the Wealth of Nations*, Volume I, London: Penguin Books, 1999.

SMITH, Helen, *Masculinity, Class and Same-Sex Desire in Industrial England, 1895-1957*, Basingstoke: Palgrave Macmillan, 2015.

SORKIN, Andrew Ross, *Too Big to Fail: Inside the Battle to Save Wall Street*, London: Allen Lane, 2009.

SPARGO, John, "Private Property and Personal Liberty in the Socialist State," *North American Review*, June 1909, Volume 189, Number 643, pp.844-856.

SULLIVAN, T. D., *The Dock and the Scaffold: The Manchester Tragedy and the Cruise of the Jacknell*, 1868, Dublin: Leopold Classic Library, 2015.

SWIFT, David, *A Left for Itself: Left-wing Hobbyists and Performative Radicalism*, Winchester: Zero Books, 2019.

TARN, John Nelson, *Five Per Cent Philanthropy: an account of housing in urban areas between 1840 and 1914*, Cambridge: Cambridge University Press, 1973.

THERBORN, Göran, in "Dreams and Nightmares of the World's middle classes," in *New Left Review*, 127 Second Series, July/August 2020, pp.63-87.

THOMPSON, E. P., *The Making of the English Working Class*, London: Victor Gollancz, 1963.

— 1975, *Whigs and Hunters: The origin of the Black Act*, London: Allen Lane, 1975.

— "Eighteenth-Century English Society: Class Struggle without Class?" *Social History*, Volume 3, Number 2, May, 1978, pp.133-165.

VAROUFAKIS, Yanis, *Another Now: Dispatches from an Alternative Present*, London: The Bodley Head, 2020.

VERCELLONE, Carlo, "From Formal Subsumption to General Intellect: Elements for a Marxist Reading of the Thesis of Cognitive Capitalism," *Historical Materialism 15*, 2007, pp.13-36.

VRIES, Jan De, and WOUDE, Ad Van Der, *The First Modern Economy: Success, failure, and perseverance of the Dutch economy, 1500 -1815*, Cambridge: Cambridge University Press, 1997.

WALDRON, Jeremy, "What is Private Property," *Oxford Journal of Legal Studies*, Volume 5, Number 3, Oxford: Oxford University Press, 1985.

WALLERSTEIN, Immanuel, "The West, capitalism, and the modern world system," in Timothy Brook, Gregory Blue (eds.) *China and Historical Capitalism: Genealogies of Sinological Knowledge*, Cambridge: Cambridge University Press, 1999.

WALVIN, James, *The Zong: A massacre & the end of slavery*, New Haven: Yale University Press, 2011.

WEN ZHENHENG, *Treatise on Superfluous Things*, circa 1615-1620, published in an English translation by Tony Blishen as *The Elegant Life of the Chinese Literati*, Shanghai: Shanghai Press and Publishing Development, 2019.

WILDE, Oscar, *The Soul of Man Under Socialism*, 1891, London: Penguin, 2007.

WILLIAMS, Eric, *Capitalism and Slavery*, Chapel Hill: University of North Carolina Press, 1945.

WILLIAMS, Raymond, "Advertising: The Magic System," 1961, in *Problems in Materialism and Culture*, 1980, London: Verso, 1997.

CULTURE, SOCIETY & POLITICS

The modern world is at an impasse. Disasters scroll across our smartphone screens and we're invited to like, follow or upvote, but critical thinking is harder and harder to find. Rather than connecting us in common struggle and debate, the internet has sped up and deepened a long-standing process of alienation and atomization. Zer0 Books wants to work against this trend. With critical theory as our jumping off point, we aim to publish books that make our readers uncomfortable. We want to move beyond received opinions.

Zer0 Books is on the left and wants to reinvent the left. We are sick of the injustice, the suffering and the stupidity that defines both our political and cultural world, and we aim to find a new foundation for a new struggle.

If this book has helped you to clarify an idea, solve a problem or extend your knowledge, you may want to check out our online content as well. Look for Zer0 Books: Advancing Conversations in the iTunes directory and for our Zer0 Books YouTube channel.

Popular videos include:

Žižek and the Double Blackmain
The Intellectual Dark Web is a Bad Sign
Can there be an Anti-SJW Left?
Answering Jordan Peterson on Marxism

Follow us on Facebook
at https://www.facebook.com/ZeroBooks and Twitter at https://twitter.com/Zer0Books

Bestsellers from Zer0 Books include:

Give Them An Argument
Logic for the Left
Ben Burgis
Many serious leftists have learned to distrust talk of logic. This is a serious mistake.
Paperback: 978-1-78904-210-8 ebook: 978-1-78904-211-5

Poor but Sexy
Culture Clashes in Europe East and West
Agata Pyzik
How the East stayed East and the West stayed West.
Paperback: 978-1-78099-394-2 ebook: 978-1-78099-395-9

An Anthropology of Nothing in Particular
Martin Demant Frederiksen
A journey into the social lives of meaninglessness.
Paperback: 978-1-78535-699-5 ebook: 978-1-78535-700-8

In the Dust of This Planet
Horror of Philosophy vol. 1
Eugene Thacker
In the first of a series of three books on the Horror of Philosophy, *In the Dust of This Planet* offers the genre of horror as a way of thinking about the unthinkable.
Paperback: 978-1-84694-676-9 ebook: 978-1-78099-010-1

The End of Oulipo?
An Attempt to Exhaust a Movement
Lauren Elkin, Veronica Esposito
Paperback: 978-1-78099-655-4 ebook: 978-1-78099-656-1

Capitalist Realism
Is There No Alternative?
Mark Fisher
An analysis of the ways in which capitalism has presented itself as the only realistic political-economic system.
Paperback: 978-1-84694-317-1 ebook: 978-1-78099-734-6

Rebel Rebel
Chris O'Leary
David Bowie: every single song. Everything you want to know, everything you didn't know.
Paperback: 978-1-78099-244-0 ebook: 978-1-78099-713-1

Kill All Normies
Angela Nagle
Online culture wars from 4chan and Tumblr to Trump.
Paperback: 978-1- 78535-543-1 ebook: 978-1-78535-544-8

Cartographies of the Absolute
Alberto Toscano, Jeff Kinkle
An aesthetics of the economy for the twenty-first century.
Paperback: 978-1-78099-275-4 ebook: 978-1-78279-973-3

Romeo and Juliet in Palestine
Teaching Under Occupation
Tom Sperlinger
Life in the West Bank, the nature of pedagogy and the role of a university under occupation.
Paperback: 978-1-78279-637-4 ebook: 978-1-78279-636-7

Malign Velocities

Accelerationism and Capitalism

Benjamin Noys

Long listed for the Bread and Roses Prize 2015, *Malign Velocities* argues against the need for speed, tracking acceleration as the symptom of the ongoing crises of capitalism.

Paperback: 978-1-78279-300-7 ebook: 978-1-78279-299-4

Meat Market

Female Flesh under Capitalism

Laurie Penny

A feminist dissection of women's bodies as the fleshy fulcrum of capitalist cannibalism, whereby women are both consumers and consumed.

Paperback: 978-1-84694-521-2 ebook: 978-1-84694-782-7

Babbling Corpse

Vaporwave and the Commodification of Ghosts

Grafton Tanner

Paperback: 978-1-78279-759-3 ebook: 978-1-78279-760-9

New Work New Culture

Work we want and a culture that strengthens us

Frithjoff Bergmann

A serious alternative for mankind and the planet.

Paperback: 978-1-78904-064-7 ebook: 978-1-78904-065-4

Sweetening the Pill

or How We Got Hooked on Hormonal Birth Control

Holly Grigg-Spall

Has contraception liberated or oppressed women? *Sweetening the Pill* breaks the silence on the dark side of hormonal contraception.

Paperback: 978-1-78099-607-3 ebook: 978-1-78099-608-0

Ghosts of My Life
Writings on Depression, Hauntology and Lost Futures
Mark Fisher
Paperback: 978-1-78099-226-6 ebook: 978-1-78279-624-4

Why Are We The Good Guys?
Reclaiming Your Mind from the Delusions of Propaganda
David Cromwell
A provocative challenge to the standard ideology that Western power is a benevolent force in the world.
Paperback: 978-1-78099-365-2 ebook: 978-1-78099-366-9

The Writing on the Wall
On the Decomposition of Capitalism and its Critics
Anselm Jappe, Alastair Hemmens
A new approach to the meaning of social emancipation.
Paperback: 978-1-78535-581-3 ebook: 978-1-78535-582-0

Enjoying It
Candy Crush and Capitalism
Alfie Bown
A study of enjoyment and of the enjoyment of studying. Bown asks what enjoyment says about us and what we say about enjoyment, and why.
Paperback: 978-1-78535-155-6 ebook: 978-1-78535-156-3